Unconditional Love:

Pet Tales to Warm the Heart

Brian J. Lowney

DEDICATION

This book is dedicated to my late parents Catherine and Thomas Lowney for affording my brother Glenn and me the privilege to own so many wonderful pets through the years. Their love and encouragement will never be forgotten and always will serve as an inspiration for my work.

TABLE OF CONTENTS

INTRODUCTION

Imagine what our lives would be like without our pets, the furry, feathered and finned creatures who bless our lives with unconditional love and fill our days with humor, joy and sometimes even with plops and puddles.

But who cares about accidents? That's why we have paper towels!

I credit my late mother Catherine for introducing me to the wonderful gift of family pets. As a very young boy, I had a colorful parakeet named Joey, whose claim to fame was that he could ride his toy bicycle a few inches across the kitchen table. Then there was a succession of small green turtles, purchased at the local five and dime store.

Once my mother discovered the presence of field mice in the neighborhood, we had to have a cat. For the past 50 years our family has seldom been without one of these magnificent creatures, each with a unique personality and a big paw print that remains forever etched on my heart.

And, of course, then came the dogs.

Annie, my first canine, was a Basset-Beagle mix, born on a local farm, who lived to be an elderly hound, but never lost her knack for stealing toys and boots from neighbors' yards whenever she managed to bolt out the door to enjoy a trip around the neighborhood.

Years later, my mother attended a dog show hoping to find a Basset Hound breeder. When she discovered a Kerry Blue being exhibited in the terrier group, her Irish heart was forever stolen and within a few months, Connolly of Castletown arrived in our home. Ironically, I had searched all over the country for a puppy and read dozens of magazines searching for information about the legendary breed; the small pup was born just two miles from my home on the other side of town.

Even though Connolly never became a champion and earned only eight single points, he introduced me to the wonderful sport of dogs and the world of dog shows. My next two Kerries did become champions, an adventure that look me to new places and enabled me to develop friendships with dozens of interesting folks from all walks of life but who all shared a love of dogs and dog shows.

Never did I ever dream that when I first was invited to submit a magazine feature about the history of junior showmanship almost 20 years ago, it would eventually lead to a weekly newspaper column, countless magazine assignments, and a new career as a journalist.

It has been an incredible adventure filled with wonderful people, many of whom, sadly, are now gone, and countless treasured animals who have crossed the Rainbow Bridge.

For many years, local readers have asked me to compile some of my columns from the past into book form. Finally, here it is. Enjoy!

CATS BRING MANY BLESSINGS

Although veterinary experts and cat fanciers across the nation have proclaimed September as Happy Cat Month, most feline owners will admit that their furry friends are always contented, especially at mealtime.

Mickey, my nine-year-old tiger cat, loves baked chicken and dances in front of the oven whenever he captures the scent of a roasting bird. He patiently sits by his dish, ignoring his usual bowl of dry food, and waits until a few choice morsels of white meat appear on the plate.

Needless to say, the hefty feline always cleans his dish, before trotting off to find a comfortable spot to curl up for a long nap. Life is good!

I have owned cats for more than 50 years, but my family usually adopted young kittens. One exception was Miss Kitty, who landed on our doorstep one day about 40 years ago, starving and ready to give birth. My kindhearted late mother Catherine nursed the frail young calico back to good health and prepared a maternity unit for the expected litter.

Another family favorite was Smokey, a longhaired grey tomcat I brought home from college in New Hampshire some 35 years ago. The handsome cat truly loved our family and purred with delight whenever someone stooped to pat him on the head.

Last year, my beloved tigress Daisy died at age 18 after bringing many years of joy and offering unconditional love to our family, but never to other pets. She simply did not like other animals and usually let them know with a loud growl and a litany of hisses.

After being diagnosed with bladder cancer six years ago, my mother underwent several surgeries and a long period of chemotherapy and radiation. Daisy never left her side except to eat and visit the litter box. When my mother had the strength to go outdoors, the sleek tigress would walk around the yard, never leaving my mother's side.

The intuitive cat had an important mission to accomplish and never stopped showering unconditional love right up to the moment my mother died with her beloved feline friend sitting by the bed.

My mother used to joke that Daisy did indeed enjoy nine lives because every time the fragile creature would become sick or get injured and it looked like the end was near, she'd bounce back in a few days with good veterinary care and lots of loving attention.

"Healthy cats are happy cats," writes Steve Dale, a Chicago-based dog and cat behavior consultant, syndicated newspaper columnist and national correspondent for *USA Weekend.*

He writes, "While some owners may dread a trip to the veterinarian with their cat, many veterinary practices are cat-friendly or have doctors who specialize in cats and will gladly show leery owners how pleasant a trip to the veterinarian can be."

Dale emphasizes that if a cat has not yet been spayed or neutered, this is an important step to keeping a cat happy and healthy; it will help prevent aggression and decrease the risk of cancer.

Although Daisy could be aggressive toward other pets and occasionally chased large dogs out of the yard, one of the friendliest and most docile cats I ever owned was Sugar, a Maine Coon, who died two years ago.

Sugar also provided my mother with lots of unconditional love and companionship, and she shared my mother's love for scones. The matronly feline relished dried cranberries and raisins, and would often jump up onto the kitchen table while my mother was reading the morning paper, steal a chunk of scone, and make a mad dash down the hallway, leaving a trail of crumbs in her wake.

The disobedient cat would hide under a bed until the coast was clear, and then would suddenly appear at the kitchen table a few minutes later, begging for another tidbit of dried fruit. It was impossible to stay angry because Sugar was absolutely beautiful and equally charming.

During Happy Cat Month, veterinary experts and animal shelter coordinators are urging prospective cat owners to adopt an older cat. Mickey is the first mature cat who I ever adopted, and it was a good choice since he was litter box trained, fastidious and well mannered when he arrived at his new home two and-a-half years ago.

The mackerel tabby loves people — he has never met a stranger — and continues to make folks laugh and warm hearts with his quirky antics, loud meows, and abundant unconditional love.

ALPACAS TURN HOBBYIST INTO ENTREPRENEUR

Plants and animals have always been a passion for David Rose so it's no surprise that the former agriculture inspector now owns one of the region's most successful alpaca herds.

The lifelong Swansea, Massachusetts resident started Moonlight Rose Alpacas more than 11 years ago, after retiring from the United States Department of Agriculture. He began with a foundation of seven colorful alpacas and now owns a herd of 68 animals: 34 of each gender.

Rose became interested in these furry creatures, which he describes as "a smaller cousin" to the llama and camel, after seeing a magazine advertisement and visiting some farms.

"Alpacas," he adds, "are physiologically similar to goats. They have their own personalities." He adds that some alpacas are friendlier than others, but these animals of South American origin are usually docile and not as aggressive as llamas.

Some farmers train llamas to serve as guards, but alpacas are prized for their luxurious fiber, which Rose takes to a Fall River, Massachusetts mill where it is spun into yarn to make gloves, hats, scarves, sweaters, socks and other apparel. The animals are shorn once a year, usually in late April.

The farmer-entrepreneur sells the fashionable, all-natural items at farmers' markets throughout the region and online. Coarser fibers are made into felt that's used to line winter boots.

"The colder the winter, the faster the fiber grows," Rose reveals, adding that because the past winter was unseasonably warm, there will be less fiber available for spinning this year.

According to Rose, 22 colors are recognized by the National Alpaca Association, a registration body similar to the American Kennel Club. All of Rose's alpacas are registered and blood typed, which enables him to carefully plan breedings according to pedigrees. The gestation period for alpacas is 11 months, and Rose discloses that multiple births are rare.

"Alpacas have the unique ability to stop labor," Rose says, revealing that females often resume the delivery once a bad storm passes. Alpacas range in price from several hundred to a few thousand dollars, depending on their quality.

The respected alpaca breeder adds that these unique animals were introduced to the United States from Peru in 1986, and today more than 175,000 of them live throughout the country. He notes that there are about 40 alpaca farms in Massachusetts alone.

Alpacas are indigenous to the Andes and are raised in several South American countries by herdsmen who also use the fiber to make clothing and blankets.

Rose notes that most alpacas stand about five feet high, about a foot shorter than a llama. Males weigh about 200 pounds, and females tip the scales at 150 pounds. The animals are generally healthy and live 15 years or longer.

Several of Rose's animals have won ribbons at exhibitions where they are judged on their conformation and the quality of their fiber.

Alpacas generally enjoy good health; they eat hay, grass and a small amount of grain. Although the animals are given a vitamin supplement, Rose reveals that too much protein in an alpaca's diet will thicken the fiber, making it less valuable. The animals require an annual rabies shot and regular worming, and must have their toenails and teeth trimmed at regular intervals.

To safeguard these valuable animals, the farm is protected by a flock of 22 guinea hens, which rid the premises of mosquitoes, ticks, grubs and other potentially harmful insects.

"They go around and eat all the parasites," Rose says. "They scan the area, and they are watchdogs."

The alpaca fancier emphasizes that despite their size, they have few defense mechanisms other than to shriek, kick, spit or run. When angry or frightened, an alpaca will spit, emitting an odiferous mixture of regurgitated grass mixed with saliva. When it sees a possible predator, an alpaca releases a high-pitched warning, a signal for the entire herd to flee and run to the barn.

The farm's most recent addition is Oliver, a handsome three-year-old Great Pyrenees rescue who was found last fall wandering on Long Island, emaciated and suffering from heartworm. Rose adopted him in December from a Long Island, New York animal shelter.

"We are working our way to be friends," Rose quips, adding that the huge white flock guardian canine enjoys supervised visits to the barn on a leash. Now that the handsome dog's health has been restored, Oliver can look forward to watching over the herd of beautiful alpacas and the squawking hens that grace the impressive farm.

For more information about the alpacas or related products, visit www.moonlightrosealpacas.com.

INSPIRATIONAL BOOKS HELP PET OWNERS COPE WITH LOSS

The loss of a beloved family pet can be a devastating experience that requires time for emotional healing and the support of compassionate family members, friends and co-workers.

Although some people once considered grieving for a deceased animal to be inappropriate, today there are support groups for owners who've lost a treasured furry or feathered companion and beautiful sympathy cards to acknowledge pets that have crossed the Rainbow Bridge.

Just as they would for any other family member, many folks are no longer ashamed to express their feelings and discuss the loss of a special animal who offered years of unconditional love and forged an unbreakable bond that can never be broken.

Popular author Christine Davis, whose charming books, which are filled with inspirational messages and whimsical illustrations, have consoled grieving owners for almost two decades, reveals that a vision of a beautiful angel moved her to write her first book, *For Every Dog an Angel*, following the death of Martha, a 50-pound black Poodle-mix who was born in the author's bathroom.

Davis subsequently wrote two other books, *For Every Cat an Angel* and *Forever Paws*, to offer hope to bereaved owners that they will one day be reunited with their furry or feathered companion for all eternity.

"It was the sighting of an angel that put me on the track," the Portland, Oregon-based writer continues, adding that her books are written "from the heart to the hearts of people who are grieving the loss of a beloved friend."

Davis tells grieving animal lovers not to be afraid to express their emotions, and to always treasure the many wonderful times that they shared with their pet.

"A large part of our journey with grief is sharing stories," she continues. "Sometimes just telling another person about your beloved critter — their name, how they came to you, all the special times you shared — can be healing."

The respected writer and illustrator encourages people who are grieving the loss of any animal "to give voice to their stories as a way of celebrating their critters and remembering all the joyful memories." She suggests sharing the poignant tales with a trusted friend or family member, counselor, or in a pet-loss support group guided by someone who understands the great void left by the death of a family pet.

"Even writing down your stories just for your own eyes can be cathartic," Davis says.

According to Dr. Thomas Burns of Veterinary Associates of Cape Cod in South Yarmouth, Massachusetts, helping children cope with the death of a pet is "one of the greatest silver linings to the pain of pet loss."

The small-animal practitioner adds that although death and loss are two of the most difficult life lessons to teach children, helping young family members to productively deal with the loss of a pet offers them an opportunity to learn to mourn in a healthy way.

"This loss can have a lifetime impact on our children's understanding and their ability to cope with loss," Burns notes. "By discussing their loss honestly, encouraging expressions of feelings, and memorializing our pets in a proper way, we can make the experience ultimately a positive one."

For more information about Davis' books, visit www.lightheartedpress.com.

DISABLED DUCK TEACHES VALUABLE LESSONS

Lemon is certainly one lucky duck!

When the tiny creature was hatched five years ago, everyone doubted that the little duckling would live more than a few days, but Lemon has beaten all the odds and matured to become a big happy duck who inspires and brings joy to everyone she greets.

"She was a beautiful shade of lemon when she was born," says the bird's owner Laura Backman, a reading specialist in the Portsmouth, Rhode Island public schools.

The Crested Pekin duck suffers from neurological issues that prevent the animal from balancing, standing or walking normally. Most veterinarians who have examined Lemon attribute the duck's condition to brain damage caused by the large crest.

Lemon was one of four ducklings hatched during a classroom science project. Backman and her students realized within a few days that although Lemon looked and quacked like a duck, the tiny bird couldn't move around like her siblings.

"She kept falling over," Backman remembers, adding that the students took turns watching Lemon at recess time while the little duck played in the grass. The teacher says that the children worked together to make the duck thrive.

By caring for Lemon, the students shared in her triumphs and defeats and learned about love and acceptance. Most important, the children discovered that disabilities and differences don't make a person or animal less special or valued.

The enchanting duck continues to visit classes and teaches students that although some people face significant challenges, they still can enjoy a happy life if they are loved and respected.

Last year, one of Backman's students, Joanna Lewis, who is hearing impaired, developed a special bond with the loveable bird.

"She could relate to the duck," reveals Susan Lewis, the young girl's mother. "It was good to see that there was an animal with a disability."

Lewis recalls that although her daughter was once ostracized and mocked, when the students began to care for Lemon after entering Backman's classroom, they became more compassionate and accepting, and began to reach out to Joanna.

"They all bonded and they didn't see the differences in their classmates," Lewis notes.

Backman and her feathered friend routinely visit schools, summer camps and programs for children and adults with special needs, and they also volunteer in the Pets & Vets program that teaches compassionate animal care and promotes the human-animal bond in inner-city schools.

"While some may consider Lemon a classroom friend or mascot, she is as much a teacher as is Laura," wrote Dr. Ted White, past president of the Rhode Island Veterinary Association in a letter praising the popular duck. "As a teacher, Lemon has inspired students and symbolized equality among able-bodied students and students with disabilities. ... In this age of classroom, playground and cyber bullying, Lemon represents the goodness of the human spirit and the warm and nurturing environment we, as parents, want classrooms to embody."

In honor of her amazing companion, Backman has written a charming children's book, *Lemon the Duck*, beautifully illustrated by Laurence Clemet-Merle of France. The book is available at www.amazon.com/.

To learn more about Lemon, visit www.lemontheduck.com.

WAYWARD AIREDALE'S PERSISTENCE PAYS OFF

Max is probably the luckiest — and most recognizable — dog in Rhode Island!

The amazing six-year-old Airedale survived a death-defying adventure four years ago, and has since bounced back to become a popular canine celebrity who constantly attracts legions of fans and eager photographers of all ages.

According to the fortunate creature's owner, Bill Clark of Coventry, the celebrity canine is best known for riding throughout Southern Rhode Island and Eastern Connecticut strapped into the sidecar of his owner's sporty black and green Honda motorcycle.

When he's out riding, the flashy terrier sports a black rhinestone-studded collar, a bright bandana and a pair of "doggles" that protect the dog's eyes and make him look just like a movie star!

"People always wave and take pictures," reveals Clark, a retired registered nurse. He adds that the dashing terrier, whose breed is the largest member of the group of dogs that were developed to hunt vermin, intrigues visitors from all over the world.

With the handsome pooch comfortably strapped into a matching sidecar painted to complement Clark's bike, the pair can often be found driving down Route 95 toward Connecticut, enjoying the beauty of Mystic or riding along quiet country roads in rural Rhode Island and over the border in the Nutmeg State.

Life today couldn't be better for the beloved Airedale, but things haven't always been so good.

Four years ago, during a leisurely autumn ride through picturesque Sterling, Connecticut, a motorcycle that had crossed the median at a very dangerous curve struck Clark's yellow Porsche convertible.

Max was sitting loose in the back seat and quickly escaped following the impact.

Luckily, there were no serious injuries, but the prized sports car was totaled and Max was gone!

"He fled into the woods," Clark recalls, sadly. "I could see him far in the distance but he just kept going into the woods."

Respondents to the accident scene helped the distraught dog owner search for hours to no avail. One man immediately posted an advertisement on a missing pet recovery service and Clark eventually returned home late that night to wait.

In the ensuing days, the distraught owner created and displayed dozens of posters, and knowing that Airedales have a keen sense of smell, even left a trail of clothing with his scent hoping to lure the errant canine back to Rhode Island.

Meanwhile, Max's breeder in Connecticut brought another Airedale, a large male named Rocket, for Clark to bring to Sterling to help coax Max from the deep woods.

When Clark arrived at the scene of the escape, Rocket acted more like his namesake than a dog and also bolted into the dense forest.

A few hours later the bewildered dogs' breeder arrived and called both names. Rocket came running out of the dense brush, but Max was still nowhere to be found, so Clark, now quite worried and burdened with a heavy heart, trudged home.

Within a few days, the frustrated dog owner began to receive calls from people who'd seen the poster or the Internet post.

"I could see where he was getting closer to home," Clark says, adding that the reports indicated that the delightful dog had crossed the Rhode Island border and was diligently searching for his owner.

Exactly 24 days following the accident, Clark returned home from an early morning shopping trip to buy more poster board only to find Max playing in the back yard.

"You can imagine how I felt," Clark emphasizes. "He came running and knocked me over."

An emergency veterinary checkup revealed that Max had lost 11 pounds during the long ordeal and his thick black and tan fur was infested with ticks. Eventually Max was diagnosed with Lyme Disease, and Clark credits Dr. Linda Tobiasz of Tiogue Animal Hospital in Coventry for helping restore the terrier's health.

The distance from Clark's house to the spot where the dog went missing is about 16 miles, but the grateful owner estimates that the large terrier in reality traveled about 45 miles, according to the calls and e-mails he received and the fact that at one point, Max was traveling in the wrong direction.

Max's incredible tale gained regional and national attention after local TV stations and newspapers reported the dog's heartwarming story. The notable Airedale was profiled in *Oprah* magazine in a feature about real life miracles, and Clark and his canine sidekick were invited to appear with Jay Leno but unfortunately could not make the broadcast.

Clark says a canine behaviorist attributed Max's safe return to the dog's sharp memory and astute powers of observation, since the pair had taken the same route to Sterling dozens of times. Airedales, by nature, are keenly intelligent and good hunters, qualities that also helped the dog to find its way home.

"He's absolutely a joy," Clark concludes as he straps Max into the sidecar before setting out on a new adventure.

4-H KIDS SURELY LOVE THEIR DOGS

For the past 22 years I have enjoyed the privilege of judging Junior Showmanship classes at American Kennel Club licensed dog shows held throughout New England and occasionally in distant states such as Virginia and Missouri. Judging these classes not only allows me to see a variety of beautiful dogs, but also to observe the great talent that our young dog handlers possess as they expertly present their canine charges in the ring.

Shortly after I began judging, I received a call from the late Al Kirby, a top-ranked professional handler, trainer and owner of Stonehouse Kennels in Westport, Massachusetts. He asked me to substitute for him at a 4-H match in New Hampshire, and told me it would be fun judging assignment and a great learning experience.

When I arrived at the show, I quickly learned that the 4-H competition, called Fitting and Showmanship classes, was very different than those I was accustomed to judging. I was surprised to see mixed-breed dogs allowed in the ring. Much to their credit, several young handlers exhibited family pets adopted from a local shelter.

Another major difference was that I could ask the young handlers up to three questions about canine anatomy and their dog's breed. In the case of a mixed-breed canine, the handler was allowed to choose which ancestor to discuss.

I was impressed by each handler's enthusiasm and ability to artistically present his or her dog to its best advantage, which is often no small feat when exhibiting a mixed-breed dog. Every animal was neatly groomed, with a brushed coat, trimmed nails and clean teeth and ears.

The competitors were judged, as they still are more than 20 years later, on their ring presentation, cleanliness and condition of the animal, knowledge of canine anatomy, breed knowledge, and whether their attire was in compliance with the prescribed 4-H uniform.

Kirby was correct. I enjoyed my assignment, made some wonderful friends, and have been judging 4-H competitions throughout the Northeast for the past two decades. One of the exhibitors at my first 4-H assignment, Sarah Gardner, now coordinates many of the competitions.

On a recent brutally hot July Sunday morning, I had the opportunity to judge 25 young 4-H handlers at the Stratham Fair in Stratham, New Hampshire. The talented exhibitors represented several local clubs scattered across the Granite State, and are eagerly preparing to compete at the Eastern States Exposition — the Big E — which is held every September in West Springfield, Massachusetts.

The most difficult part of my assignment was judging the senior class, which had 19 entries and several highly skilled competitors. Many of these young dog fanciers also compete at AKC events, exhibiting in the conformation ring as well as junior showmanship, rally and obedience.

I have judged at Stratham many times, so some of the older kids knew what I was looking for as they presented their dogs. Others remembered suggestions I had made during past assignments and worked diligently to show me how much progress they had made since last year when I judged at the popular fair.

Most of the handlers — even the very young ones — possess a fundamental knowledge of canine anatomy and can usually answer my questions, but what always impresses me most is the handlers' knowledge of breed origins and development. I was fascinated by one participant's knowledge of Viking history and the ancient

Nordic breeds that were the ancestors of the Norwegian Elkhound, the breed the young woman was exhibiting that day.

One of the more unusual exhibits was a long-coated Whippet, which at first glance I thought was a Borzoi-cross. The handler explained that the variety is widely recognized in England, where the Whippet was developed as "the poor man's Greyhound." These smaller but very agile racing dogs were prized by factory workers, who entered their canines in Sunday races that became great sporting events for the working classes. In this country, the Whippet is popular as a lure courser. For those who aren't aware, lure coursing is a sport that involves chasing a mechanically operated lure.

After making a flawless presentation with the handsome Whippet and answering my questions, the exhibitor earned a perfect score of 100 points. Another handler, presenting a beautifully groomed Shetland Sheepdog, also could not be faulted, so there was a tie for first place.

After both handlers successfully completed a series of difficult ring patterns, I knew that I somehow needed to break the tie. Since the 4-H classes had studied the sporting breeds that year, I asked the two finalists which pointing breed had just been admitted to the miscellaneous class by the AKC and much to my amazement, the young lady exhibiting the Sheltie replied, "the Wirehaired Vizsla."

After winning the large class, the young handler continued her stellar performance by defeating the winners of the other divisions, and eventually took home the top prize: a large purple rosette.

OUCH! PAINFUL ARTHRITIS ALSO AFFECTS OUR PETS

Do you have trouble getting out of bed or stooping down to pick up the morning paper?

Like millions of folks, you may be suffering from arthritis, a painful disorder caused by the inflammation of one or more joints. Medical researchers report that there are more than 100 different forms of arthritis, and most patients are able to manage their pain with prescription drugs, physical therapy and other forms of treatment.

According to veterinary experts, painful arthritis also affects many of our companion animals.

"Arthritis is more often noticeable in dogs, but cats also suffer from arthritis much more often than many owners realize," begins Dr. Tom Burns of Veterinary Associates of Cape Cod in South Yarmouth, Massachusetts.

Burns says felines are more adept at hiding signs of sickness and pain, and often an owner will only notice subtle signs when the condition is moderate or severe.

Nationally-syndicated pet columnist and author Steve Dale says that some obvious signs that a cat may be suffering from arthritis include a hesitancy to jump up on counters, and repeated failure to travel up and down stairs to use a litter box.

"Cats don't generally tell us," Dale reveals, adding that it's much easier to detect arthritis in dogs when they limp or have difficulty walking even a short distance.

Burns, a graduate of Tufts University's Cummings School of Veterinary Medicine, notes that osteoarthritis, which occurs when joint cartilage wears down, often occurs at a much earlier age in canines than their owners might expect, with many cases being diagnosed between four and seven years of age.

He adds that osteoarthritis is a degenerative disease and includes progressive discomfort, muscle atrophy, and overall decrease in limb function and quality of life.

"Usually it is secondary to development of hip or elbow dysplasia, obesity, and other common orthopedic conditions," Burns tells. "It is also not unusual to see dogs beginning to exhibit signs of arthritis as early as one to two years of age."

Veterinary experts agree that it's important for owners to take early signs of arthritis seriously, when the disease is mild and treatment options are more effective and less expensive.

Burns adds that although owners often attribute a new limp or stiffness to getting older, in reality, "age is not a disease. While we all have a few aches and pains, many more dogs and cats live in chronic pain than need to, and can easily and effectively be treated," Burns shares.

"Sometimes the most telling early signs include a pet's stiff gait upon rising after a long rest. If your pet commonly limps after sleeping, arthritis or other orthopedic conditions should be suspected."

There is no cure for arthritis. Burns says that the most effective treatment plans are multimodal, using a combination of treatments rather than one single modality. He reports that this allows for lower overall dosing of medication, often decreasing the potential side effects of any one treatment.

"The goal of treatment is improve quality of life and slow the progression of the disease," Burns emphasizes. "Much of the pain associated with arthritis can be controlled, so often there is no reason to let a dog or cat live in chronic pain without treatment."

The small-animal practitioner discloses that weight management of overweight pets is considered by most veterinarians to be the single most clinically effective and cost effective treatment for arthritic pets.

"Not only does extra fat place excessive forces on the affected joints, it produces pro-inflammatory mediators, making the condition even worse," he says, advising that there are many options for medications and therapies to make pets more comfortable and slow the progression of the disease.

Burns notes that laser therapy is the one of the newest technologies, providing a pain free and noninvasive treatment that has recently complimented multimodal care but without pills.

According to the veterinarian, the infrared laser beam is targeted right to the painful region or affected joints with virtually no side effects.

"The cost of laser therapy is often less than many clients expect, and usually no sedation is required," Burns concludes, adding that physical therapy is also beneficial to many arthritic patients, helping them lose excess fat, increase muscle tone, and provide better range of motion.

Dale, the author of two new e-books, *Good Dog* and *Good Cat* (Tribune Media Services), says that it's important for pets to visit their veterinarian twice a year and for cats and dogs whose arthritic pain is managed to receive regular exercise to keep them active.

He suggests that cat owners engage their feline friends in feather play, and move food to different locations around the house to stimulate activity, and advises owners of larger canine breeds — such as retrievers — to allow their dogs to enjoy an occasional swim — if Fido likes the water.

"Exercise is very important," Dale emphasizes. "The good news is that there is a lot owners can do to help their pets that suffer from arthritis."

SPECIAL CAT INSPIRES DELIGHTFUL BOOK

Some pets are truly unforgettable and leave an indelible paw print on their owner's heart.

For Warwick, Rhode Island author Kristen Dyer Calenda and her husband Tony, that animal was Nubiana, a petite longhaired black cat with sparkling yellow eyes, a small pink tongue and a great big heart.

Calenda readily admits that the gentle feline changed the couple's lives forever and she chronicles the heartwarming story of that special bond in a charming book for children of all ages entitled *Nubiana: A True Story About a Very Special Kitty.*

Nubiana's saga began in January 2006 when Tony's friend, who was moving, asked him to surrender the cat to an animal shelter. Luckily for the couple, Tony forgot all about the request and brought the small cat home, secure in her crate in the back of his red pickup truck.

"Nubiana came at a time when I had no use for cats," the author recalls, adding that since it was a weekend and the local shelter was closed, the abandoned feline was temporarily housed in the garage and left to sleep on an old bath towel that had been placed in her crate.

The next day was sunny, so the curious cat was brought outdoors to explore the garden. Word of her arrival spread quickly throughout the neighborhood, and one family who visited the Calendas agreed to adopt the disheveled, homeless cat once she was properly vaccinated, bathed and groomed.

Once Nubiana received a medical checkup and a spa treatment, the Caldendas couldn't let go of their precious gift and decided to give the beautiful cat a loving home.

"Nubiana was a Persian cat," Calenda writes in the book. "Her face was as flat as a pancake. Her nose was flat, too, with two tiny holes for her to breathe from. That cute little nose sat high, almost between her eyes. Oh, those eyes! How they just made you melt like ice cream. How beautiful she was!"

"She was so exquisite," the author recalls. "People didn't think she was real. I never heard her cry."

Calenda adds that Nubiana "brought comfort to everyone she met" and liked people.

"She was a healing cat," Calenda continues. "I could see how people were transformed when they held her in their arms."

In the captivating book, beautifully illustrated by noted artist Susan Shorter, Calenda recounts the feline's adventures throughout New England, either sitting in a stroller or being carried in a tote bag, but always enjoying the ride and attracting a crowd of curious onlookers who were captivated by the magical feline's beauty.

The tale also reveals how Nubiana transformed her adoptive parents into cat owners. In December 2006, the Calendas acquired Oscar, a black male Persian who still volunteers as a hospice cat, and have since adopted two other felines who fill their home.

Sadly, just as quickly as Nubiana entered the Calendas' lives, she suddenly departed early one morning in May 2008.

"I heard a mourning dove cooing," the writer recalls, adding that since all the windows of the house were shut, she went downstairs to see whether a bird had entered the home, only to find Nubiana's lifeless body under a chair. Oscar was sitting at his feline friend's side.

"Nubiana was sent to me for a reason," Calenda reveals, adding that she was inspired to write the book after taking classes at All That

Matters, a yoga and holistic education center in Wakefield, Rhode Island where instructors "lit the fire" that fueled her to put pen to paper and write the enchanting tale.

The author adds that the inspirational story teaches many valuable lessons about love and kindness, travel and adventure, togetherness and parting.

"It's a heartwarming story of a special bond and relationship that forever changed and fulfilled lives," Calenda says.

Partial proceeds from book sales benefit animal-related and other local charities, such as hospice programs. Calenda often appears for book signings at charity events and libraries, and shares her love of writing and Nubiana's charming story during school visits.

Nubiana: A True Story About a Very Special Kitty is available at bookstores throughout the state, on Amazon or from the author's website at www.kristencalenda.com.

POODLES GO PINK FOR A CURE

Four local dog fanciers and their troupe of stunning Poodles are helping make a difference in the lives of women struggling with cancer.

Acushnet, Massachusetts residents Jim and Laurie Rollins, her sister Heidi Nunes and mother, Joan Brenneke, both of Dartmouth, Massachusetts, and their Breast Cancer Awareness Poodles have been bringing smiles to folks of all ages while raising awareness of the disease at venues all across Southern New England since October. They plan to continue the important project that brings hope to many women and their loved ones.

The project began when Laurie Rollins decided to honor Nunes, a cancer survivor for 10 years, and celebrate Breast Cancer Awareness Month by dressing her two chocolate standard Poodles, Gertrude and Gretel, with pink feathers in their ears and topknots and coloring the pom-poms at the end of their tails with bright pink non-toxic chalk.

"I'm always looking for new places to put feathers," Rollins begins, adding that she formed the nine-member canine troupe by adding her mom's four Poodles, known affectionately as "The Irish Boys," together with Nunes' three dogs, "The Farm Boys."

"We call Gertrude and Gretel 'The Cocoa Puffs,'" she says, referring to the dogs' luxurious chocolate-colored fur. The lively canine group includes all three Poodle varieties — toy, miniature and standard.

When Rollins and her mother decided to surprise Nunes by "pinking" the Poodles several weeks ago and lining them up on a deck to be photographed, they never expected that the project would be so much fun.

"It was a big surprise," recalls Nunes, who cried as Poodles of all colors and sizes danced around her. For the special occasion, the Rollins' and Brenneke's well-behaved dogs sported bandanas inscribed *In honor of Aunt Heidi*. The message on Nunes' dogs' scarves read *In honor of Mama*.

Nunes says the family event planted the seeds to begin a fundraising project that would benefit women facing struggles similar to those she has witnessed, while enabling the Poodle fanciers to share the joy and unconditional love that the dogs offer every day.

The sisters decided to take some of the dogs to WaterFire in Providence, Rhode Island, which held a special "Flames of Hope" event on October 6 that attracted thousands of spectators from all over Southern New England.

"It was amazing," Rollins says. "That's when we noticed the power of the pink Poodle."

Nunes adds that countless spectators stopped to ask about the handsome dogs, take pictures and share their own stories of how cancer has affected their lives.

According to Nunes, who works as a medical transcriptionist, her Poodles have always been a great comfort, especially when she suffered three life-threatening bouts of cancer more than a decade ago.

"It's always in the back of your mind," Nunes reveals, adding that she undergoes a routine checkup every six months, and now is in good health.

Following the success of their Providence adventure, the Poodle devotees visited Boston, Provincetown and Newport, where for a small donation, they presented folks with a "Paws for a Cure" postcard featuring a colorful photograph of the nine dogs and an inspirational message.

"We really worked the crowd in Provincetown," Rollins reveals, adding that the well-mannered canines were "a big hit" at every appearance they made with their owners. "Everyone just loved the dogs."

To date, the amazing Poodles have raised $1,135, including donations from the sisters' friends living in this country and Canada, to support the Women's Breast Cancer Center at Women and Infants Hospital in Providence, where Nunes has been successfully treated.

The Poodle fanciers plan to make additional appearances throughout the region in the coming months and welcome invitations to raise funds for the worthy cause.

"We'd pink them out again for breast cancer," Rollins notes, adding that the enthusiastic dogs love meeting people and posing for photographs.

For more information about the Breast Cancer Awareness Poodles, visit them on Facebook at:
http://www.facebook.com/pages/Breast-Cancer-Awareness-Poodles-BCAPs/125719537585643; or contact Rollins by email: bcapoodles@gmail.com.

MILITARY DOGS ARE ALSO HEROES

As we pause this Memorial Day to honor the countless valiant American men and women who sacrificed their lives so that others could enjoy freedom, we shouldn't forget the military working dogs that have served with great loyalty and courage in battlefields throughout the world for most of the past century.

These dogs were deployed in World War I, World War II, Korea, Vietnam, the Persian Gulf, Bosnia and Kosovo, and continue to serve in Kuwait, Afghanistan, Iraq, Korea and other spots across the globe.

Military working dogs are trained by skilled soldiers to serve as scouts, trackers, sentry dogs, and to detect land mines, booby traps, tunnels and hostile forces approaching by water.

Historians estimate that these courageous canine heroes saved more than 10,000 lives during the conflict in Vietnam in the late 1960s.

"They are the eyes and ears of the soldiers, especially at night," begins Steven Luz, a former handler who served with the United States Air Force at Da Nang Air Base, one of the major installations used by American troops during the Vietnam conflict.

The retired California Highway Patrolman and Rhode Island native recalls that when a dog barked or raised its ears during a patrol, the handler needed to investigate the disturbance. Sometimes the commotion was caused by another animal rustling in the grass, or a villager walking near the perimeter of the base. Other times the intelligent war dog had detected a Viet Cong insurgent preparing to attack.

"It was up to the handler to determine if it was a threat," Luz adds. He notes that Da Nang was hit by 25 rocket attacks during the year he was stationed at the base.

He reports that although some of the dogs used in Vietnam were bred in the United States, many of the canines were whelped in Japan. Since most of the dogs were aggressive, it sometimes took several weeks and a lot of patience before the soldiers could gain the trust of their canine comrades.

"It's called 'getting in on your dog,'" Luz says, noting that a handler used a choke collar and muzzle to help control the war dog at the start of the eight-week training program.

"Taking the muzzle off is the first test," he emphasizes, adding that some of the dogs turned on their handlers.

The young soldier, originally from West Warwick, was lucky and quickly developed the trust of Rinney, a handsome German Shepherd male who served as Luz' partner for nine months.

Luz developed a strong bond with the courageous canine by "throwing a lot of love" and playing with the large herding dog. The young soldier was also responsible for grooming his canine charge.

Although Luz tried not to become emotionally attached to Rinney, he recalls the last time he saw the courageous dog.

"The day I flew back, I made one last trip to the kennels to say 'good-bye,'" Luz remembers. "It was kind of hard."

Luz is an active member of the Vietnam Dog Handlers Association and developed a website four years ago dedicated to the members of his group, the 366th Security Police K-9 Unit. Using the Internet, Luz has been able to locate 80 of his comrades, including Everett Tremblay of Swansea, Massachusetts.

"All you had to do was keep an eye on the dog," Tremblay says. "They were pretty sharp. I'd say 'watch' and he'd watch for me."

The longtime Swansea resident trained Kobuc, a sable-colored German Shepherd.

Tremblay says that the military working dogs "reflected the personality of their handler. If the handler was lazy, the dog was lazy."

Tremblay adds that the Armed Forces used German Shepherds because the breed is intelligent, loyal and has a coat that insulates the animal from extreme temperatures.

Luz says that since the military working dogs were trained to be aggressive, the animals would not have made good pets once they were retired from active duty. Most of the animals were euthanized.

President Clinton signed a law in 2000 allowing military dogs too old to continue their duty to be adopted rather than being put to death. If a dog is deemed suitable for adoption by the commander of the dog's last duty unit in consultation with the unit veterinarian, the animal will be available for adoption by law enforcement agencies, former handlers and trainers, or other individuals deemed capable of caring for the retired canine.

The law also requires anyone receiving a retired military working dog to agree not to hold the government responsible for any injury or damage resulting from ownership of the dog.

Military dogs that are not adopted or euthanized for medical reasons are sent to installations where the animals are used to train new handlers.

In her new book, *The Nightingale of Mosul*, retired Col. Susan Corry Luz, a field hospital nurse, writes about the respect these dogs have earned from their fellow soldiers. She is the sister-in-law of Steven Luz.

"One of my first patients was a dog, a severely wounded German Shepherd," she recalls, adding that the canine underwent emergency surgery after being shelled by terrorists.

"I was told, 'This dog is an American soldier.'" Sadly, the canine's handler was killed in combat.

Air Force Staff Sgt. Christopher Dion, stationed in Korea, sends the following poem via e-mail describing the bond that military working dogs and their handlers develop as they patriotically serve their country:

"May the Lord bless your walk and way,

And by your footsteps may paw prints lay,

For no truer friend is there this day,

Than the dog beside you who will forever stay."

To learn more about military working dogs, visit http://366thspsk9.com.

SALVE GRAD CAUGHT THE DOG SHOW BUG

When Mary Michaela Duffy Rein ('75) graduated from Salve Regina College in Newport, Rhode Island, little did she know that in a few years her life would go to the dogs.

Armed with a degree in Mathematics and minors in Biology and Education, the Barrington, Rhode Island native soon landed a job as a middle school math teacher at the Joseph Gaudet Middle School in nearby Middletown, where she remained for 34 years before retiring in 2009.

The popular educator, affectionately known as "Micky," settled in Somerset, Massachusetts, and soon caught "the dog show bug."

At an age when many young women's lives revolve around changing diapers and warming baby bottles, Rein's afterschool hours and weekends were spent grooming and exhibiting champion Samoyeds. She later moved to Berkley, Massachusetts, where she operated a boarding kennel for 26 years and launched a career as a professional dog handler.

During the past two decades, Rein has successfully campaigned more than 30 dogs to their American Kennel Club championships, and also exhibited in Canada and Bermuda. She's shown a variety of breeds, both large and small, for clients as well as her own dogs, which have included a top-winning Schipperke, a few Black Russian Terriers, and several Bouvier des Flandres, a large Belgian herding breed that has been her constant companion for many years.

Although Rein is retired from the formal classroom, she continues her love of teaching by instructing conformation classes at the Wampanoag Kennel Club in Acushnet, Massachusetts, and has served as president of the organization for more than a decade.

Rein now lives in Dighton, Massachusetts, and also continues to exhibit at dog shows held all over New England and Eastern Canada.

The respected dog trainer credits Salve Regina for providing her with a solid education and enhancing the strong moral values that she was taught at home by her parents, the late Vincent and Loretta Duffy.

"I liked the small community that Salve offered," Rein recalls. "It was like one big family, and I had a lot of great professors."

She fondly recalls the late Sister Mary Brenda Sullivan, RSM, who taught Anatomy and Physiology.

"She was tough, but boy, could she teach, " Rein remembers.

Another inspiring professor was the late Dr. Leo J. Bottari, who served as chairman of the Biology Department and coordinator of the Medical Technology Program before his retirement in 2001.

"His personality was such that you wanted to learn from him," Rein says of her former Biology and Microbiology professor. "He was motivating and he made it fun. Everything was so alive with him."

Rein adds that the lessons she learned in the science classrooms at Salve Regina and the respect that she was taught for life in all forms also served her well as a dog breeder.

"I think some of the things I took away from the college gave me self-confidence and made it easier to move on in life," Rein emphasizes, adding that she left the Salve Regina campus equipped with a solid education and Irish tenacity that prepared her to meet any challenge.

"Perseverance and determination pay off in the end," Rein emphasizes, noting that those qualities, which she developed at

Salve Regina, helped her enjoy a rewarding teaching career and much success in the sport of purebred dogs.

"A well-trained and obedient dog is a valued and beloved member of the family," the dog fancier shares. "They round out our lives, cheering us up when our day hasn't been quite what we hoped."

Rein describes the bond between a dog owner and his four-legged companion as "unparalleled" and one that shouldn't be taken lightly.

"You see it on the news that a dog saved its family by alerting them to danger, whether it be a fire, an intruder or sensing an oncoming health issue," she continues. "I can't imagine what life would be like without them."

The dog expert notes that although a canine's love is unconditional, humans owe these animals something in return.

"If you're going to have a dog in your house, it should be trained so it's friendly and not jumping on people and on the table, stealing food from people's plates," she says, adding that every puppy should attend a basic obedience class.

"A dog that is a good member of their family becomes a 'forever dog,'" Rein concludes. "Others end up in shelters and we know that's not a good place for them to be."

AH, THE THRILL OF WESTMINSTER!

A dapper Sussex Spaniel made dog show history by winning top honors at the 133rd annual Westminster Kennel Club dog show held Feb. 9-10, 2009 at Madison Square Garden in New York City.

Ch. Clussexx Three D Grinchy Glee, affectionately known as Stump in the dog show world because the canine has stubby legs and a shiny golden brown coat and resembles a tree stump, is the oldest canine ever to win at Westminster. The 10-year-old came out of retirement to capture his 51st career Best in Show win after suffering an almost-fatal illness caused by a bacterial infection five years ago.

According to handler Scott Sommer, the 50-pound canine quickly adapted to a leisurely life as a house pet after an extensive show career, and was only exhibited occasionally once he regained his health.

"I love them all, but tonight it's the Sussex," said Judge Sari Brewster Tietjen, as she pointed to the handsome flushing spaniel that was also the audience's choice among the seven outstanding finalists. Every time the noted arbiter glanced at Stump, the crowd cheered and broke into thunderous applause.

"He showed his heart out," Tietjen said in a later interview with members of the dog press. "I didn't know who he was or how old. ... I just couldn't say no to him."

AKC statistics for 2008 reveal that the Sussex ranked 145th out of 156 breeds in popularity, and only 74 dogs were registered. The breed was developed in England several centuries ago to flush game birds from thick underbrush.

Sometimes when an unusual dog scores a big win at the Garden or appears in a Hollywood blockbuster, its breed surges in popularity and falls into the hands of unscrupulous backyard breeders eager to sell puppies to meet the growing demand for that type of dog.

Swansea, Massachusetts resident and Sussex fancier Polly Ryan doesn't think that will happen to this old-fashioned hunting dog that has always attracted a small yet loyal following.

"People will not have the patience to wait for a Sussex," she reveals. "Breeders are very particular to whom they sell their puppies."

Ryan says several breeders have reported an influx of calls and e-mails since Stump's win, but most people just want to learn more about the breed. These dogs are expensive. Pet quality dogs cost about $1200, and show specimens usually sell for $2,000 or more. These dogs are trusting companions and excellent hunters, but prospective owners should know that Sussex Spaniels drool and shed.

The respected breeder emphasizes that Stump is a good representative of the breed and deserved the big win.

"It's very nice that a veteran dog can win like that," Ryan continues. "He looks good for his age."

Although every dog entered at Westminster didn't win a ribbon, just having a dog entered and exhibited at the prestigious event is an honor for most dog fanciers.

"It was a big show and it was very exciting," reports Winnie Kelly of Fall River, Massachusetts, whose Borzoi, Ch. Dibar's Kiss of Death "moved beautifully and showed well" in a large breed entry of 34 dogs.

"I was in the bleachers with my binoculars," Kelly reports. "I couldn't be seen by Kiss. She'd go bonkers."

The pre-school teacher and longtime dog fancier reveals that the large canine tried to escape from handler Sara Gregware several weeks ago at a show when the animal caught a glimpse of her owner chatting with friends at ringside.

"I have to hide," Kelly says. "She looks for women with short hair and glasses."

According to the well-known Borzoi fancier, exhibiting at Westminster costs a lot of money. She estimates spending about $1,000 for the services of a professional handler to groom and exhibit the champion canine, and adds that she spent an additional $200 for the one-day adventure she enjoyed in New York City.

Kelly says that despite the Westminster loss, Kiss has achieved a notable show record, including two hound group placements awarded by Borzoi breeder-judges.

"Kiss is ranked 18th in the top 20 Borzois in the United States and that's with limited showing," the proud dog fancier concludes, adding the impressive sighthound won two Best of Breed awards in Hartford immediately after the Westminster show.

LIKE HUMANS, ANIMALS GRIEVE WHEN A LOVED ONE DIES

Do animals grieve when their owner or another member of the herd dies?

Last fall, when my cat Sugar suddenly disappeared, my other feline Daisy shrieked incessantly for days until I discovered the missing feline's lifeless body hidden under a bush in a remote section of my back yard.

Once Sugar was buried, her feline housemate gradually returned to a normal routine, but still made daily trips out to the back yard to visit her friend's grave.

Most animal behaviorists and trainers agree that the majority of cats and dogs, like their human counterparts, experience grief in their own way for varying periods of time. Some pets are sad for only a few days, but others sink into a deep depression that can last for several weeks or longer.

Respected Pug breeder and exhibitor Alan Alford reveals that often times in multi-dog households a canine will mourn the loss of a special buddy.

"In my experience, dogs frequently grieve the loss of a friend. I've watched some of my dogs over the years that have bonded with another pet, sharing food and toys with that specific individual dog while never permitting some other member of the 'family' to participate."

Alford adds that some dogs, like humans, develop depression when a loved one dies.

"I've also witnessed dogs go into a depressed state when that special friend dies. The first day or two the grieving pet just wanders around looking for his buddy. By the end of the second day, the dog stops searching and just mopes around, and refuses food, play and toys."

The well-known toy dog authority says it takes most canines about a week "to return to normal" and start enjoying life once again.

"There's no question in my mind that these dogs have just passed through a grieving state over the departure of their mate," Alford emphasizes.

Marsha Pugh, a noted writer and animal expert, discloses that herding animals, such as horses, cows and sheep, form family bonds and grieve over the loss of a loved one.

"In their natural world, they would live in large family groups," she wrote in an e-mail from her Maryland home.

"If a horse is sold away from the group, the rest will whinny and neigh for weeks afterward," she discloses. "It's very traumatic to change the herd dynamic."

Pugh discloses that she had heard that elephants grieve if they can't mourn the passing of one of their deceased herd mates, so when one of her own horses died, she decided to conduct an experiment.

"When my oldest mare died, I allowed the others to see her, sniff her body and realize that she had died, not just disappeared," she writes.

Pugh notes that the mare's daughter, Dolly, was brought out of the barn to witness the burial.

"She stood over her mother until the heavy equipment came to move the body, dig her burial spot and bring her down to the site," Pugh continues. "Dolly followed the backhoe and waited patiently, standing guard until her mother was completely covered and the equipment left. From that day forward, when she was let out of her stall in the morning, the first place Dolly would go was to her mother's grave and stand over it for a few moments before moving on to graze. She is now buried alongside her mother."

Pugh reveals that cows also grieve.

"I saw my neighbor's cow give birth to a premature calf," she recalls. "It didn't live long, less than an hour. As the mother stood over her baby, trying to nudge it back to life, all the other cows gathered around. Then they formed a line and each cow walked by, gently touched the dead calf, and then moved on. It was the most amazing thing I had ever seen."

Pugh remembers that the cows also comforted the mother by gently nudging her and remained with the grieving animal for the rest of the day.

"Years later, when that same farmer's horse died and was being buried, all the cows that had been lying in the cool shade under the trees stood up and watched the burial. It was almost like they were paying respect to the dead," she adds.

The well-known animal authority advises horse owners to allow their other equines to see the deceased before it's removed or buried, because animals understand death and need to mourn the passing.

"Unfortunately, I have had to use my own advice more often than I cared to," she concludes. "Being that their lifespan is 30 years or more, you develop a close relationship with them and it's devastating when they die."

THERAPY DOGS RELIEVE STRESS DURING FINALS

The last two weeks of any semester on a college or university campus are often filled with anxiety for students as they scurry to finish projects, write papers and prepare for finals. There are lots of trips to the library, sleepless nights and jolts of caffeine before the start of summer fun.

At Bridgewater State University in Bridgewater, Massachusetts, the Health Services and Counseling Department sponsors a unique program during this taxing time by offering an Outreach Education Stress Free Zone where students can make their own stress balls, create a friendship bracelet, and be soothed by the unconditional love of man's best friend.

Ann M. Doyle, the department's outreach education coordinator, recalls that a student approached her last year with the idea to bring therapy dogs to campus. Fortunately, a faculty member was involved in pet therapy and helped facilitate the popular program.

"It's a great opportunity for the students to come in and relax," says Doyle, adding that that the hour-long sessions provide a brief respite during the last week of classes and allow the students to clear their minds and have some fun for a few minutes before they shift their attention back to their studies and the added stress of finding summer employment.

During the four-day program, a different volunteer team visited the campus daily. The canines offered lots of kisses and wagging tails. Students petted the friendly dogs, laughed with their friends, talked about their own pets and snapped photos on cell phones.

The dogs and their owners are certified for their important mission either by Therapy Dogs International, a national registry that trains qualified handlers and dogs, or by Dog B.O.N.E.S. (Dogs Building

Opportunities for Nurturing and Emotional Support), a Scituate, Massachusetts-based nonprofit organization that provides well-trained, obedient, affectionate, registered and insured therapy teams who visit nursing homes, schools, college campuses and other facilities throughout Massachusetts.

Last Tuesday, a handsome three-year-old Golden Retriever named Owen was the big man on the Bridgewater campus.

According to his owner, Robin Bradley of Marshfield, Massachusetts, the gentle dog graduated from Dog B.O.N.E.S.' intensive four-week training program last November. During the course, Owen's temperament was evaluated, and the dog was introduced to a variety of situations and equipment that a therapy dog might encounter, such as wheelchairs and walkers.

"He's a comfort dog," Bradley says, adding that Owen recently participated in a healing program at Saks Fifth Avenue in Boston in the aftermath of the Marathon bombing.

She adds that the perceptive canine is "very intuitive when people are stressed. "He's pretty laid back," Bradley continues. "He's a typical Golden Retriever."

Other dogs that participated in the university stress reduction program included a pair of Siberian Huskies, a Petit Basset Griffon Vendeen and some toy breeds.

Bradley recalls that she decided to volunteer last year after her older Golden Retriever named Cooper died unexpectedly, leaving Owen depressed and lethargic.

"He was sad over the loss of his buddy," Bradley discloses. "I wanted to get him out and do something that was just about him, and he has risen to the occasion.

"When I put on his vest, he knows that he's going out," the proud owner notes, pointing to the bright red vest emblazoned with the therapy program's insignia to indicate Owen's status as a registered therapy dog.

For sophomore Morgun Knabbe of New Bedford, Massachusetts, having a canine on campus was a welcome surprise.

"I love dogs," reveals the 2011 graduate of Greater New Bedford Regional Vocational Technical High School, who is pursuing a degree in management at Bridgewater.

Knabbe, a commuter, has a cat at home and likes to care for his sister's Mastiff.

"It's a good idea," he says of the dog therapy program.

"It's crunch time," Knabbe continues, adding that he spends a lot of time in the commuter café studying for exams and finishing term papers. Once he graduates, he plans to purchase a dog.

"I'm a German Shepherd fan," he says. "I love Golden Retrievers, too."

For Melanie Mitchell of Millbury, Massachusetts, a junior English and psychology major, Owen proved to be the perfect antidote for a stressful day.

"Animals will love you no matter who you are or what you do," she explains, noting that her family pet is a cat.

"I don't get to see animals very often on campus when I'm away from home."

EXPERTS CONTINUE TO DEBATE ANIMAL INTELLIGENCE

Are dogs smarter than cats?

Animal intelligence has been a hotly debated topic for centuries among veterinarians, behaviorists, psychologists and pet owners. Although there has been quite a bit of research done on the subject and a few books written, such as Stanley Coren's *The Intelligence of Dogs*, most experts only offer opinions that are not based on scientific research or facts.

"There is no answer to that question," begins Steve Dale, popular radio personality and syndicated pet columnist. He adds that a poll taken a few years ago revealed that 40 percent of the respondents believed that cats and dogs possess equal intelligence; 30 percent thought cats are smarter; and 30 percent said man's best friend was more intelligent than its feline counterpart.

"How do you measure intelligence?" the writer asks, noting that it's difficult to find a test that can be administered to both species since cats' and dogs' brains are programmed to perform different functions.

Dale says perhaps the smartest creature is the parrot. He tells of an African Grey that learned to call the family dog and imitate the sound of the timer on a microwave and a doorbell.

"Parrots have the ability to train us," Dale says, adding that the bird's owners finally caught on and stopped running every time the bird made a sound.

The award-winning author recalls another parrot that watched television coverage of Princess Diana's funeral in 1997 and responded "So sad, so sad" as the commentators discussed the proceedings.

"Was he repeating what he heard or comprehending?" Dale asks. He notes that scientific research has proven that most of these colorful creatures possess the intelligence of a two-year-old child, and some can differentiate colors and objects.

Swansea, Massachusetts pet owner Colleen Brown agrees that the question is difficult to answer simply because cats do not think like their canine counterparts. Brown has trained high-scoring dogs in obedience and agility.

"Dogs are considered easier to train because they have been bred and developed to respond to humans," Brown says. "Some dog breeds are more trainable — for example, sporting and herding dogs, whose continued existence depended upon their response to commands from their humans."

The Irish Wolfhound fancier reports that hounds were developed for tracking as well as chasing and running down prey.

"These dogs did not need to respond to humans as much and therefore, they have not developed the response mechanism that sporting dogs may have," Brown reports. "However, that does not say they are not as intelligent as other breeds."

Terriers, long known for the keen intelligence and sense of humor, were bred to go to ground and chase vermin.

Brown also discloses that some dogs are more intelligent than other specimens of their breed. She says she would match her wolfhound Morgan's intelligence against that of any dog, but her other dog Lorrha, although lovable, isn't as smart as many other canines.

"Generally, I think cats are better problem solvers because they have had to work to get their food and continue to exist," Brown continues. "They were not fed readily by their humans, as dogs are, so they have to think about where their next meal will come from or how they will accomplish whatever goal they have. Like dogs, when they want to be fed, they come and pester their owners to open up the cans and feed them. If one of my cats is ignored, he gets his dry food from the cupboard."

Air Force Staff Sgt. Christopher Dion, a military dog trainer serving on active duty at Kunsan Air base in Korea, has trained these intelligent canines for many years and describes them as "unsung heroes." Usually these canines are German Shepherds or one of the Belgian breeds noted for its keen intelligence and tremendous courage.

"Dogs have served in the military since the Roman legions and probably before," Sgt. Dion writes in an e-mail. "As long as dogs have been domesticated they have served man in every possible way. Their intelligence is often their best asset, but it often takes the most patient and consistent handler to bring out the best in them."

Dion, a native of Holyoke, Massachusetts, says that dogs are like children: each has its own personality. Some dogs are timid, and others are more outgoing.

"With each different personality a different training method is required," Dion concludes, noting that trainers must be constantly aware of changes in the dog's behavior and act accordingly.

"In the end, the capability of the dog is limited only by the skill and patience of the trainer and the personality and hidden talents of the dog. Just as not every thoroughbred horse is a Secretariat, not every dog is a Lassie or Rin Tin Tin."

TRAINER PERFORMS MIRACLES WITH DIFFICULT DOGS

Paul Hankins is often called a "miracle worker" or "the dog whisperer of Fall River (Massachusetts)."

Others refer to the amiable dog trainer simply as "Papa BowWow," founder of the doggie daycare and training center that bears his humorous nickname.

Although many basic obedience instructors offer classes that will hopefully teach a dog owner how to train the family pet to become to become a good citizen and a joy to own, Hankins has gone one step further; he offers a Juvenile Delinquent Class at his training facility, Papa BowWow's Doggie Daycare and Playschool, located at 505 Bay Street in Fall River.

The goal of the structured class, which is limited to a maximum of four participants, is to give owners the correct information so they can gain control of their dog.

"The alternative is euthanasia or isolation," Hankins says, adding that before a dog can enter the class, the animal must first be evaluated in its owner's home or at the training facility, and receive individualized obedience lessons to ensure that it can safely be trained in a room with other dogs.

According to Hankins, aggression is a term that is often misunderstood. He emphasizes that behavior that might be labeled by some people as aggressive — barking, growling, stiffening and making eye contact — is part of a dog's defense mechanism and mode of communicating.

Any form of aggression, however, becomes unacceptable, anytime it's directed toward a human or excessively toward another animal.

"There is no cure for aggression, but it can be controlled," Hankins emphasizes.

Since he began the J.D. program more than three years ago, Hankins has worked successfully with owners of almost 100 dogs, some of which other trainers had banished from their class or suggested that the canine be euthanized.

Class members have included mixed-breeds and purebreds, shelter dogs and canines purchased from private breeders, and dogs of all ages. The one characteristic that they all share is undesirable behavior, which Hankins says can be modified if owners are consistent, have lots of patience and a sense of humor.

"You must practice during the week," Hankins tells the owners during an early morning class held last Saturday. "Coming here for an hour is not going to work."

The certified dog trainer emphasizes that it's important that dogs learn to behave appropriately where they spend the most time, which is usually their home, and not just in training class. He tells owners to develop a "zero tolerance for bad behavior" and never to get frustrated.

The well-known dog trainer also advises owners to make sure their canine charges get plenty of exercise — "to get the stress out" — and to always praise positive behavior whether verbally or with a small food reward.

Hankins says he named the sessions as such because just as the courts send youth labeled "juvenile delinquents" for training and counseling in the hope of making positive changes, there is also hope for these dogs to become obedient and valued family members.

One of the dogs currently enrolled in the class is Rocky, a handsome Boston Terrier owned by Bob and Linda Bramwell of Westport, Massachusetts.

"I fell in love with the breed," Linda says, adding that she now owns three specimens of the breed that is the official state dog of Massachusetts.

The experienced dog owner reveals that although Rocky is usually a gentleman, the small black and white canine suffers from separation anxiety, and becomes agitated whenever someone tries to leave the Bramwell's house. Linda attributes the dog's behavioral problems, in part, to being separated from his mother at four-and-a-half weeks of age, when he was sold as a Christmas gift.

"He circles people and tries to nip at their feet," she continues, revealing that the comical canine also unties shoelaces to prevent guests and family members from leaving. Rocky is also very protective of Linda and the couple's two female Boston Terriers.

Rocky is being treated by a veterinarian with anti-anxiety medications, and is gradually demonstrating better behavior as a result of the weekly classes and daily practice sessions.

"The combination is working," Linda reveals, stating that her goal is for Rocky to live and interact successfully with his owners and canine housemates, as well as with other dogs that he meets outside of the home.

To learn more about the Juvenile Delinquent Class offered at Papa BowWow's Doggie Daycare and Playschool, call Hankins at (508) 679-1703.

JOEY PUTS AFFENPINSCHERS ON THE MAP

Few folks had ever heard of an Affenpinscher before a tiny little dog called Joey became the top banana in the dog world by winning Best in Show at the 137th Westminster Kennel Club dog show recently held at Madison Square Garden.

Grand Champion Banana Joe V Tani Kazari became an instant celebrity across the globe, captivating dog lovers of all ages with his charming personality and comical antics.

For Mattapoisett, Massachusetts resident and longtime Affenpinscher breeder Nancy Baybutt, the victory finally put her beloved breed on the map.

"It took 77 years for the rest of the world to recognize and appreciate an Affenpinscher," Baybutt begins, noting that the breed was recognized by the American Kennel Club in 1936.

Baybutt, whose Sienna Gold Kennels has produced more than 40 "Affie" champions, received more than 30 calls and e-mails from all over the country following Joey's big win, seeking information about the breed or inquiring about the availability of puppies or older dogs.

The respected breeder adds that since these dogs have small litters and because of a limited gene pool, she's doubtful that the breed will experience a surge in popularity. Baybutt notes that most Affenpinscher breeders are responsible, communicate with each other, and sell only to select homes, although she warns that some puppy mills sell unhealthy specimens that don't conform to the breed standard or haven't been properly socialized.

Most reputable breeders sell well-bred puppies for $2,500, which Baybutt says is less expensive than the cost of prolonged veterinary care for a poor specimen beset by health problems.

Baybutt, a lifelong dog lover whose father, Dr. Hugh Dailey, was a prominent Boston veterinarian and exhibitor of Wire Fox and Scottish Terriers, won acclaim in the sport of purebred dogs by breeding several generations of top-winning Golden Retrievers. She's also hunted with Viszlas and owned Cairn Terriers and Schipperkes.

The knowledgeable fancier fell in love with the Affenpinscher more than 20 years ago after spotting a beautiful young female puppy at a dog show in Saratoga Springs, New York. She purchased the dog, named it Nutek Sienna Gold Black Pearl, and exhibited the charming canine to its championship.

Black Pearl was also a star in the whelping box and was the dam of 10 AKC champions.

According to breed historians, the Affenpinscher is an ancient dog that was developed in Germany to hunt small vermin on farms, and to keep stores and homes free of mice. In German, the breed's name is translated as "monkey terrier," probably because these quick-witted canines resemble small primates.

The official breed standard emphasizes that although these dogs are small, they are not delicate. Described as a dog of medium bone, the Affenpinscher should ideally measure between 9 ½ and 12 ½ inches at the withers, and according to Baybutt, most specimens weigh about six pounds or a little more.

Known for its outgoing personality, the Affenpinscher is generally quiet but does bark when provoked or excited, as Joey was when the crowd at the Garden went wild when Best in Show judge Michael Dougherty pointed to the well-groomed canine.

"The Affenpinscher is a very smart little dog," Baybutt continues. "It likes to venture out. It's curious and friendly." She reveals that females like to hunt and always seem to have their nose to the ground, but males, like Joey, are more affectionate.

"Males are lovers," she quips. "They totally concentrate on you. They can cuddle one moment and then go on a two mile walk."

With proper training and a very patient handler, Baybutt says these dogs excel in performance activities such as obedience and agility.

The distinguished breeder admits grooming the wire-coated dogs is not her forté, but she does enjoy exhibiting young dogs just starting their show careers.

"I love going into the ring with a puppy," she says.

After owning Affenpinschers for more than two decades, Baybutt has become a widely recognized expert on the breed and tells folks not to be fooled by the toy dog's size.

"They are in every way a big dog," she concludes.

PET TOY BUSINESS IS ALL IN KNOTS

When Capt. Dave Bill was a young boy and learned to tie knots, little did he know that his new interest would someday take him to faraway places and lead to the creation of a unique pet toy company.

The 51-year-old nautical science instructor at Tabor Academy in Marion, Massachusetts combines his passion for knot tying with his love for dogs and cats to produce Island Time Pet Toys, an exclusive line of all natural, nautical themed playthings made from cotton rope and twine.

"I've pretty much been a water rat since I was a kid," the Marion resident begins, adding that he grew up on Long Island Sound in Connecticut. "My mom tells me that I would crawl down to the water's edge and eat sand as an infant."

After high school, Bill pursued mariner training at a Merchant Marine school in Maryland before working on ships in South and East Africa, South America and Northern Europe. After obtaining his captain's license, he worked aboard sailing yachts in the Caribbean.

The respected seafarer eventually returned to land and joined the Tabor faculty in 1989. A few years later, he earned a Master of Marine Affairs degree from the University of Rhode Island.

Bill then started Island Time Sailing School, named after the Caribbean notion of letting things flow a natural course. His sidekick at the time was a seagoing yellow Labrador Retriever named Ceilidh who loved to play with pieces of line taken from boats that her owner sailed.

"I took a look at the pet toy marketplace and quickly found that most of the pet toys available are made overseas and none of them are made with any care or of natural, quality materials," Bill explains. "I thought, 'Wouldn't it be cool to use traditional rope to create nautical style dog toys?'"

With his daughter Tayler sitting on his lap, Bill launched Island Time Pet Toys in 1999, and he makes each knotted plaything by hand. The pet-loving entrepreneur creates five different nautical themed toys for dogs, and two for cats.

The toys not only provide pets with hours of fun, but also motivate cats and dogs to exercise as they toss and chase the fibrous amusements.

"I go with the best all natural materials I can find," he reveals, adding the dog toys are made from cotton grown in South Carolina. Cat toys are created using thick braided cotton Seine twine.

According to Bill, one of his best-selling products is the Dognut, a canine toy shaped like a rope doughnut and available in standard and puppy sizes.

Another favorite is the 2-Bites, a bone-shaped rope toy made with a traditional hand-sewn nautical eye splice on each end.

"The cat toys are a big hit," Bill observes, adding that the Cat's Paw toy, a six-strand monkey's fist hand tied around a one-inch jingle bell at the end of a 30-inch rope cord has won rave reviews from cat owners.

Bill reports that all new dog toy products are tested by his dog Ben, a nine-year-old Pembroke Welsh Corgi who serves as the company's "chief executive dog," and new cat designs must first meet with the approval of littermates Flash and Magic, a pair of handsome tomcats.

"The cats will just sit at the table and watch me make the toys," he adds. "They're fascinated by the movement."

Bill emphasizes that although safety is a top priority when creating a new product, the toys are not indestructible. Owners should always monitor their pets to ensure that the toys, like all other playthings, are not pulled apart and ingested.

For now the toys are available in a few select local pet stores, but Bill hopes to expand incrementally through Internet sales.

"It's a cottage business," he discloses. "I'm someone who likes to be productive. "

Bill says he makes the toys at night while watching TV or sitting in the doctor's office.

"I have a bag in which I carry my materials," he reveals, laughing. "It's very much like knitting."

The active pet lover adds that it takes determination and patience to create the rope toys.

"It takes a certain work ethic to stick with it," Bill concludes.

For more information about Island Time Pet Toys, visit www.islandtimepets.com or call (508) 748-1148.

COULD YOUR PET BE SUFFERING FROM DEMENTIA?

Does your dog wake up in the middle of the night and pace back and forth in a frenzy?

Perhaps your cat scratches up a storm in its litter box, and then relieves itself on the kitchen floor.

Although these behaviors may be caused by underlying medical conditions, the family pet could also be suffering from dementia, or "cognitive dysfunction" as the condition is called in veterinary medicine.

According to Dr. Thomas M. Burns of Veterinary Associates of Cape Cod in South Yarmouth, Massachusetts, there is no known cause of this progressive disease.

"Among the suspected culprits is vascular damage leading to hypoxia in the brain, beta-amyloid plaques in the brain, oxidative stress or modification of proteins in the brain," Burns discloses. Hypoxia occurs when a particular region of the body is deprived of an adequate oxygen supply.

The respected veterinarian reports that companion animals are now enjoying longer lives, thanks to improvements in veterinary care and nutrition.

"With an increasing senior pet population, we are seeing more pets with apparent dementia," Burns continues, adding that one veterinary study revealed that more than 25 percent of cats ages 11 to 14, and more than 50 percent of felines age 15 and older experienced at least one senior onset of a behavioral problem.

"In dogs, cognitive dysfunction can develop as early as age 10," he says. "However, it is usually seen in dogs that are older."

Burns notes that published data shows that some prescription medications may be helpful in slowing the progression of the neurological disease. He adds that veterinarians traditionally prescribe Selegiline or Anipryl for both cats and dogs, although newer drugs, such as Senilife and Novofit have helped pets benefit and may be used together.

"There is some anecdotal evidence that diet can help early to moderate cognitive dysfunction," the veterinarian states, adding that he is unaware of any definitive study that's been conducted to determine whether nutrition affects the progression of the disease.

Burns reports that Hill's, a leading manufacturer of pet foods, produces Prescription Diet Canine Brain Diet, a specifically formulated dog food developed with a blend of antioxidants and other nutrients such as Omega-3 fatty acids to fight the symptoms associated with cognitive dysfunction and advancing age.

"Veterinarians first must rule out underlying medical conditions that could mimic the clinical signs of cognitive dysfunction," Burns emphasizes. He lists kidney or liver diseases, high blood pressure, arrhythmias, and a reduction in vision or hearing as examples of medical conditions often found in senior dogs that mirror signs of cognitive dysfunction.

"Only after a thorough senior evaluation that includes laboratory work and testing — such as blood pressure — can a patient be considered to have cognitive dysfunction," Burns says. "There is no definitive test for cognitive dysfunction. It is diagnosed by exclusion of other medical conditions."

Pet writer and radio talk host Steve Dale says the symptoms of cognitive dysfunction are similar to those found in humans. He uses the acronym DISH (disorientation, interaction, sleep, housetraining) to explain the debilitating condition.

For example, when a dog is disoriented, the canine seems confused, forgets the location of its food dish and knocks into furniture.

Affectionate dogs suffering from some form of dementia might suddenly withdraw and become socially isolated, or once shy and reserved canines want to interact with their owners by begging for attention and becoming unusually vocal.

Like many humans suffering from cognitive dysfunction, dogs may also experience changes in their sleep-wake cycle. It's not uncommon for these canines to anxiously pace back and forth during the night when the rest of the family is trying to sleep.

A housetrained dog that frequently barks to be let outside, then quickly returns and urinates on the kitchen floor or living room rug might also be experiencing cognitive dysfunction.

Like Burns, Dale says it's crucial for cats and dogs to be examined every six months to rule out physiological causes for behavioral changes.

The popular author says it's important for owners to keep their canines active to help prevent the onset of the neurological disease.

"Keep your dog in training," he advises, adding that exercise not only keeps a dog mentally alert, but also in good physical condition.

Dale also suggests that owners purchase a wooden puzzle that will challenge canines to use their problem-solving skills to move pegs to find treats.

"Begin before they get old and cognitive changes set in," he urges.

Dog book author and medical writer Lexiann Grant reports that Wylie, her 15-year-old Norwegian Elkhound, is suffering from cognitive dysfunction and requires a great deal of care.

"Wylie has also become very difficult to groom," she laments. "We have to muzzle and sedate him to trim his toenails and even regular brushing stresses him terribly. He becomes anxious, pants and often just falls down. He always tries to get away."

Grant describes the elkhound's behavior as a "huge change" for the former showdog.

"He used to jump on the grooming table when we told him 'table' and would stand for a couple of hours being prepped for the ring."

EMERALD ISLE IS HOME TO MANY DOG BREEDS

St. Patrick's Day is not only a great day for the Irish, but also a wonderful occasion to celebrate the many fascinating dog breeds that originated on the Emerald Isle.

Ireland is the ancestral home of the regal Irish Wolfhound, handsome Irish and Irish Red and White Setters, the sporty Irish Water Spaniel, and four noble vermin hunters: the Kerry Blue, Soft Coated Wheaten, Glen of Imaal, and Irish Terriers.

According to historians, the earliest reference to the Irish Wolfhound appeared in Roman records in the late fourth century. These large dogs were often given by royalty as gifts, and were used to hunt Irish elk, guard flocks of sheep and serve as family companions.

Swansea, Massachusetts resident Colleen Brown has owned Irish Wolfhounds for more than 15 years. She trains her dogs in obedience and rally.

"Irish Wolfhounds are very gentle, very strong and sometimes very mischievous," begins Brown, adding that these dogs are the tallest of the hundreds of breeds registered by kennel clubs throughout the world.

"They sometimes like to play games with their owners," she continues, noting that the loyal sighthounds are keenly intelligent and, like most Irishmen, have a playful sense of humor. Brown adds that her hounds sometimes like to dig holes in the back yard, then fill them with bones and favorite toys and make her guess where the treasures are buried.

Brown's Irish Wolfhounds have earned many performance titles, but she admits that training them does require a lot of perseverance and the patience of St. Patrick.

"They do not like repetition," she says, explaining that to prevent her dogs from getting bored as they train for obedience and rally trials, she often "adds a new twist" to each training session to keep the hounds interested and focused on the various routines that a canine must complete to earn a leg on a performance title.

The official AKC breed standard notes that these dogs measure 32 inches or higher at the withers (shoulders), and usually weigh about 120 pounds. Sadly, Irish Wolfhounds suffer from a variety of health issues, including bone cancer, and most enjoy a short lifespan of only six to eight years.

"Wolfhounds are great dogs but they are not for everyone," Brown notes, explaining that since a national dog food manufacturer has recently been featuring an Irish Wolfhound in its commercials, interest in the breed has skyrocketed. She says although these loyal and loving dogs are accurately portrayed, the public needs to know that Irish Wolfhounds require a lot of room, regular exercise and at least a weekly brushing. Wolfhounds can be expensive to keep since most have good appetites, and especially if long-term veterinary care and medication is required to treat a medical condition.

For more information about the breed or events, contact the Irish Wolfhound Club of America at www.iwclubofamerica.org/, or the Irish Wolfhound Association of New England at www.IWANE.org.

One of the most popular of all the Irish canine breeds is the Soft Coated Wheaten Terrier, believed to be an ancestor of the Kerry Blue Terrier, which resulted from the mating of Wheatens with blue-colored dogs that swam ashore when the Spanish Armada sank off the West Coast of Ireland in the late 16th century.

Legend tells us that Wheatens were prized hundreds of years ago by Irish farmers as skilled vermin hunters because of the breed's great stamina and keen intelligence. Although a well-bred Wheaten won't back down from an opponent, these canines are the most laid back of all terriers and make great family companions.

Perhaps the Irish breed with which I am most familiar is the Kerry Blue. I went to my first dog show 33 years ago in search of a Basset Hound puppy, and decided to let my late mother Catherine tag along. She fell in love with the first Kerry Blue she spotted, and like all Irish mothers, she got her way. A few months later, one of these lively canines arrived at my house and quickly stole everyone's heart.

We named the curly little puppy Connolly of Castletown after Bishop Connolly High School in Fall River and my late father Tom's ancestral home in Ireland. Like most Irishmen and all terriers, Connolly had a stubborn streak, but was always very loyal and very protective of my father, who was later crippled by Parkinson's disease and confined to a chair for most of the day.

A good pint of Guinness, a lively jig, and these wonderful Irish breeds are all part of the Auld Sod's great legacy. Happy St. Patrick's Day!

RESCUED JACK RUSSELL BRINGS JOY TO NEW OWNERS' LIVES

Elliott Clark just might be the luckiest dog in town.

The handsome Jack Russell Terrier not only celebrated his 20th birthday on March 9, 2010 but also found a loving new home eight years earlier after being relinquished by his previous owners, who wanted to euthanize the deaf canine.

That's when New Bedford residents Andy and Susan Clark came to the rescue and decided to give the enthusiastic little vermin hunter a second chance. It was probably one of the best decisions that the compassionate couple ever made.

"I had my heart set on getting a Jack Russell," says Andy. "I wanted a Frisbee dog, the kind I could take to the beach."

Clark adds that the couple had just gotten married and purchased a small home in 2002 when he started searching on the Internet for a Jack Russell. A rescue group informed him that a Rhode Island family was searching for a new home for their dog. When the Clarks visited Elliott they learned that the friendly canine had been born deaf and was 12-years-old.

"He ran right to us," Clark recalls. "We decided to take him."

The dedicated dog owner says that since Elliott spent much of his earlier life confined to a crate, the enthusiastic canine had no problem adjusting to playing in a fenced-in yard, and being taken for long walks around New Bedford's Buttonwood Park and car rides to the post office.

"I took him everywhere I went," says Clark, "I just threw him in the car. It made up for lost time."

The intelligent terrier quickly won the hearts of the couple's friends, who enjoyed watching Elliott's amusing antics, such as playing with a blue rubber ball and pursuing the family feline.

"We took him home and right off the bat he started chasing the cat," Clark continues, adding that Cane, the couple's tomcat, and Elliott immediately bonded and remain good pals.

The proud dog owner reveals that Elliott is probably one of the oldest dogs in the area, and calculates that the canine just reached his 100th birthday in human years. Veterinary experts report although most dogs age at a rate of seven years for every one human year, the ratio decreases as canines grow older.

Clark admits that although Elliott has slowed down a bit, the charming little terrier still has a good appetite.

"As soon as my wife gets home, he follows her around the kitchen, begging for whatever she's cooking," Clark chuckles. "He's a character and he's got his own personality."

The Jack Russell fancier reveals that the biggest challenge he's faced since Elliott was adopted is remembering not to leave the front gate open. The precocious dog likes to escape and explore the neighborhood, but he can't hear approaching vehicles. Luckily, the curious canine has escaped being injured when he takes an occasional trek down the street.

"He's wanders like a goat trying to graze," Clark says, laughing. "He reminds me of an old goat."

The enthusiastic dog owner adds that although one veterinarian told him a few years ago that Elliott would soon be crossing the Rainbow Bridge, another small-animal practitioner said that the canine was in generally good health and would beat the odds.

Advanced age has caused the dog's brown markings to turn white, and Elliott often has halitosis, a condition that is remedied with doggie breath mints.

"He still has elasticity in his muscles," Clark notes, adding that the veterinarian suggested that Elliott be given an aspirin daily to relieve joint pain caused by arthritis. An occasional swim in the family pool in warmer weather also helps to keep the healthy animal in good physical condition.

Clark says that Elliott celebrated the milestone birthday with some steak and a cup of doggie ice cream. The dog received one additional gift — his own Facebook page — and attracted more than 100 fans within a few days.

Although the humorous little terrier has lived a long and colorful life, Clark hopes that Elliott will stay around for a couple of more years and break a record or two.

"He's pretty much part of the furniture," Clark says of his canine sidekick. "To not see him would be rough."

JUDGING ASSIGNMENTS LEAD TO NEW DISCOVERIES

One of the greatest pleasures that I receive from being a dog show judge is traveling to new places and meeting interesting people of all ages.

Awhile back, I had the opportunity to judge at the Three Rivers Kennel Club All Breed Dog Show held at the Purina Event Center in Gray Summit, Missouri. My assignment included judging Junior Showmanship classes and the Puppy Sweepstakes at the Kerry Blue Terrier Club of St. Louis specialty show.

I had hoped for a larger entry, but the three young Kerries that appeared in the ring were truly excellent specimens of the Irish breed that I had owned and exhibited for more than two decades. The eventual winner, Sandollars Xmas Rock Star, born just last December, immediately caught my eye when he stepped into the ring.

This young terrier has an impressive long head, dark eyes and a short back, three attributes of a well-bred Kerry Blue. The handsome dog moved effortlessly and never let his handler down, a testament to the excellent training he'd received from his breeder-owner-handler.

Another attribute that caught my eye was the young dog's luxurious plush coat, which was groomed to perfection. Unlike the hard-coated terrier breeds — such as Welsh, Airedale and Wire Fox, which are hand stripped — the Kerry Blue, with its soft curls, is laboriously scissored by hand. Grooming any terrier coat is truly an art and takes a lot of patience and practice.

Following the judging, I was happy to learn that my choice for the pink and green Best in Sweepstakes rosette had finished his Canadian championship at the age of six months.

Although Rock Star appeared to be tired and bored in the regular classes after the sweepstakes judging, and probably just wanted to go back to his crate and take a long nap, the handsome terrier was the big winner the following day, winning points toward his championship and several brightly-colored ribbons.

The other highlight of my Missouri assignment was judging the Junior Showmanship classes. Most of the young participants in these classes can outperform experienced adult handlers, so the competition is keen and often very difficult to judge. I often have to split hairs when making placements because the junior handlers do such an excellent job of presenting their canine charges correctly according to the breed standard.

My winner exhibited a Standard Schnauzer with the skill of a professional handler and I later read that the young lady repeated the big win the next day.

Anyone who exhibits dogs in conformation or obedience, or who is a member of a dog club, will readily testify about how difficult it is now to find a venue to hold a dog show. Show sites are quickly disappearing as indoor arenas are closing as a result of the faltering economy, and outdoor locations, such as school athletic fields, are becoming too costly to rent. Fortunately, the people at Purina developed an event center on the pet food company's expansive, well-maintained farm 40 miles west of St. Louis.

The large exhibition hall offered well-lighted, spacious rings, with custom-textured sports flooring that was easy on the dogs', exhibitors' and judges' feet. In addition, there was a large dining room, the Checkerboard Café, located ringside, where judges could eat without having to waste half of their lunch break walking across expansive show grounds trying to find the dining area.

Located in the heart of the United States, it's no wonder why this prime location is the site of many national breed specialties and dozens of all-breed and obedience competitions.

In July, I also had the privilege of judging the 4-H Fitting and Showmanship classes at the Stratham Fair in New Hampshire. Unlike AKC competitions, participants in 4-H shows are questioned and scored on their knowledge and presentation skills.

Many of the dogs exhibited in 4-H are mixed-breed family dogs with long histories that were adopted from animal shelters and skillfully trained by their young handlers. Training any dog is an arduous task that requires patience and determination, but it is truly an accomplishment to successfully teach one of these dogs with an often less than favorable past to become a treasured member of the family and a responsible canine good citizen.

DAISY FILLED OUR HEARTS WITH JOY

The death of a treasured pet is a difficult loss to bear, especially if the cat or dog has been a member of the family for many years.

Two weeks ago, Daisy, my beloved elderly tiger cat, died suddenly one morning in the garden. She finished a light breakfast and went outdoors to rest in a shady, secluded spot where she often lay while my mother Catherine busily tended to the colorful flowers and blueberry bushes that she planted decades ago.

For many years, Daisy often patrolled the backyard garden, chasing intruding canines, swatting bugs and butterflies and hunting plump field mice, which were often deposited on the doorstep as a gift for my mother.

Our veterinarian suspects that the 18-year-old feline suffered a heart attack, which he attributed to old age.

When Daisy arrived at our Swansea home, the tiny creature fit snugly into the palm of my mother's hand. At just six weeks old, the Mackerel tabby already had a ferocious appetite that she never lost.

The playful kitten was a 30th birthday present for my brother Glenn, and although she was not a replacement for my late father Thomas, who had died a month earlier, the delightful creature helped ease our sorrow by offering unconditional love and lots of hearty laughs.

Daisy immediately bonded with our two Kerry Blue Terriers, Connolly and Jacqui. At first, the two inquisitive canines were bewildered by their new housemate, but soon were bemused by her antics and would chase the energetic feline around the house before my mother stopped the ruckus.

Daisy seldom missed an opportunity to enjoy a good meal, but she particularly enjoyed Thanksgiving and Christmas celebrations. The curious cat ran into the kitchen once she smelled the aroma of roasted turkey wafting through the house, and danced in front of the oven until the big bird was taken out to cool. My mother always served Daisy a few pieces of cooled turkey and the giblets before our family sat down to enjoy our festive holiday dinner.

The beloved feline also relished New Year's Eve, which she celebrated with a few deveined large Gulf shrimp to mark the special occasion.

Several years ago, Daisy suddenly disappeared one day and couldn't be found. My mother was frantic and searched for hours but could not find the missing cat, who seldom left the yard.

The next morning, my startled mother looked out the breezeway window and saw Daisy crawling up the driveway, desperately trying to get home. The ailing feline was in shock and covered with bite marks and dried blood.

My mother immediately put on rubber gloves, wrapped Daisy in a fluffy towel, and rushed the distressed animal to the veterinarian, who told my mother that he'd try to save the wounded animal but could make no promises. Daisy was rushed into surgery and then placed in a supervised unit where her progress could be monitored. We were told it would be several days before the lucky cat could come home — if she survived — and be placed in quarantine.

Much to my mother's surprise and joy, she received a call from the veterinarian the following morning. He told my mother that Daisy began screeching for food once the anesthesia wore off and several hours later had just finished eating a hearty breakfast. Since the demonstrative feline didn't like being confined to a small cage, the medical staff suggested she be supervised at home.

"This is the cat that has nine lives," the vet said, laughing, when we brought Daisy for a follow-up visit a few days later.

Daisy could never have been crowned "Miss Congeniality," but the statuesque tiger cat truly loved my mother. That was evident when my mother, suffering from kidney cancer, became bedridden shortly before her death four years ago.

Daisy rested patiently at the foot of the bed, and occasionally would get up and gently kiss my mother's arm or forehead before going back to her post. When it became time for hospice intervention, Daisy tried to protect my mother and had to be removed from the room.

Minutes before my mother slipped away, Daisy stood on her hind legs, placed her front paws on the hospital bed that had been placed in the living room and stared at my mother for several minutes. It was the loving cat's way of saying good-bye to her good friend.

Now they are together again.

VIZSLAS ADD SPICE TO OWNERS' LIVES

Most dog fanciers will readily admit that they've never met a Vizsla that they didn't like.

These affable, affectionate Hungarian Pointers are not only attractive, but can also easily adapt to most any living situation, whether it be a city apartment or a country home. All these dogs need is an owner who is willing to devote time for daily exercise, proper socialization with people and other creatures, and just like any other canine, sufficient training that will enable these handsome sporting dogs to become treasured family companions and responsible canine good citizens.

New Bedford, Massachusetts residents and longtime Doberman Pinscher owners Len and Rita Gadomski were introduced to the Vizsla a few years ago at an obedience class and were immediately impressed by the breed's many fine qualities.

"It caught our fancy," Len begins. "They are a friendly dog, nice looking and easy to care for."

The Gadomski's interest in the versatile hunting breed, which excels in the field as well as in the performance and conformation rings, led to the purchase of a puppy that they named Aldebaran's Pride, Gadomski's Archie, affectionately known as Archie.

The 20-month-old dog, exhibited by professional handler Jamie Donelson, recently became an AKC champion, and under the Gadomski's tutelage, also earned a Companion Dog (C.D.) degree in the obedience ring.

Owning dogs that excel in obedience is nothing new for the couple, who have been active in that sport for the past 35 years and whose Dobermans set many records that have yet to be broken. Len, a retired manufacturing engineer, now serves as an obedience instructor at The Dog Paddle Pet Food Store, Grooming and Training Center in Bourne, Massachusetts.

"You meet a lot of nice people," he says, recalling that an exhibitor who enrolled in an obedience class at the center introduced him to the ancient sporting breed that was developed by Magyar hunters to work with falcons on Hungary's grassy plains.

The couple was so impressed with Archie's early success and handsome appearance that they later purchased a young female, Cinnibar's Choice, Gadomski's Lacy, whom Rita trains and will exhibit in the obedience ring while her husband works with Archie to obtain advanced obedience titles.

"We hope to become record breakers in Vizslas like we were in Dobermans," Len reveals.

He describes the Vizsla as "reasonably intelligent" and adds that these muscular dogs are ideally suited for performance activities because they are athletic, enthusiastic and like to please their owners.

"They are an 'up' dog," he continues. "They are very active."

The Gadomskis also like the fact that these short-coated dogs are easy to maintain and don't require a lot of grooming, like its cousin, the Wirehaired Vizsla, which has an inch-long coat. Although seldom seen in this country, the wirehaired variety was admitted into the miscellaneous class last year by the AKC and can now be exhibited at shows.

Breed experts explain that early hunters developed the wirehaired cousin by crossing a Vizsla with a German Wirehaired Pointer to produce a dog that could hunt during winter and inclement weather when the short-coated dogs needed to be kept indoors.

According to breed historians, the Vizsla was developed more than 1,000 years ago to hunt upland game such as grouse and quail, rabbits and waterfowl, since these dogs are also excellent swimmers and have a keen sense of smell.

Despite these admirable qualities, the Vizsla's popularity eventually waned during the second millennium and the breed almost became extinct at the beginning of World War I. After the conflict, a small band of dedicated European fanciers began a breeding program, and interest in the versatile breed slowly increased during the 20th century. The Vizsla was first imported to the United States in the early 1950s and was admitted into the AKC in 1960.

The breed's most outstanding physical characteristic is its rich, solid golden-rust color that, when combined with its swift, effortless movement, makes a Vizsla a standout in the sporting group and a frequent winner.

Although the Vizsla is the smallest of the pointing breeds, with an ideal male measuring 22 to 24 inches tall at the withers, these dogs do have big hearts.

"They just like people," Len explains. "They just bounce off the walls for attention. If there was a wolf or a lion, I think they'd try to make friends with it."

Rita adds that the dogs enjoy a long walk at night and often attract a lot of attention.

"People confuse them with Weimaraners," she explains, noting that many folks stop and ask questions about the dogs and the breed.

The Gadomskis agree that the dogs are a good hobby and keep them focused and healthy.

"A lot of people retire and end up watching TV, " Len says. "The dogs are keeping us active."

OWNING A DOG CAN BE EXPENSIVE

Pet experts reveal that although the cost of raising a dog is certainly not as expensive as bringing up a child, it's important for prospective owners to have the financial resources necessary to provide for the animal during its lifetime.

Research is key, they add, noting that owners should understand a breed's particular health issues as well as feeding, grooming and training requirements before making a purchase. In addition, owners should be financially prepared to cover routine long-term medical and preventive care and incidentals, such as vacation boarding, toys, leashes and a travel crate.

Third generation Labrador Retriever breeder John Cappelina, owner of Forecast Labradors in West Barnstable, Massachusetts and president of the Cape Cod Kennel Club, reports that most experienced, knowledgeable Lab breeders get $1,500 for a well-bred, healthy puppy of either gender that can serve as an ideal family companion and, if the owner chooses, can also be exhibited in the show ring or trained for a variety of performance activities.

He notes that most healthy Labs can enjoy a lifespan of about 14 years.

Cappelina, who also owns and exhibits champion Pointers, adds that puppy buyers often pay the same price for a dog born in a respected kennel as they would from a backyard or inexperienced breeder who doesn't have adequate knowledge of health problems, genetics and training.

"Puppies want to learn," he emphasizes, adding that the ideal age to enroll young dogs in puppy kindergarten is 10-12 weeks.

Cappelina notes that the cost of a basic obedience course should cost a dog owner about $150-$200.

"Trying to train an untrained dog is hard," he continues, adding that some owners wait to begin training a dog until the animal is six- or eight-months-old, after the canine has already developed bad habits and enjoys testing its master.

"If you put the time in during the first year, you'll have a dog you want to live with," he emphasizes.

Cappelina says one of the many good things about Labs is that these loyal sporting dogs require little grooming. He reveals that an occasional swim will keep a retriever clean.

Frequent bathing, he reveals, causes the coat to lose important oils, which results in hair loss.

The experienced kennel owner and exhibitor says it costs about $5,000 for a show quality Lab to earn its championship. As a result of the poor economy and rising fees, entries at dog shows are rapidly declining and it's becoming very difficult to earn championship points, which are based on the number of dogs entered in a particular breed at a dog show. Instead of pursuing conformation titles, many owners are entering their dogs in performance activities, such as rally, agility and obedience.

Dr. Tom Burns of Veterinary Associates of Cape Cod in South Yarmouth, Massachusetts, says it's always advisable to bring a new puppy to a veterinarian within a few days of introducing the animal to its new home.

"Having a thorough physical exam will ensure that your new four-legged family member is entirely healthy and preventative care can begin as soon as possible," he says.

According to Burns, a young puppy's first veterinary visit is slightly longer than a routine exam; it gives a veterinarian time to pass along important information about caring for their new furry family member.

"Beyond vaccinations, we discuss nutrition, flea and tick control, heartworm prevention, as well as proper behavior skills," he continues. "This first visit is a good time to answer any questions the client may have about their new puppy."

Burns adds that the puppy will need to be examined again three to four weeks after the initial visit. During the second visit, a veterinarian will administer another round of vaccinations and once again discuss nutrition, flea and tick control, heartworm prevention and proper puppy behavior.

The respected animal practitioner says that the average cost of these initial veterinary visits and treatments ranges between $75 and $175.

For owners not interested in exhibiting or breeding dogs of exceptional quality, veterinary experts recommend spaying or neutering the animal. Burns says that on average, a dog owner should expect to pay $300 to $500 for a canine spay, and $250 to $350 for a canine neuter.

"We strongly encourage our clients to consider having their pet microchipped during these surgical procedures, which typically adds another $50 to the fee," he adds. A microchip is a permanent form of identification and helps law enforcement and animal shelter officials return lost canines to their owners.

Burns reports that according to figures supplied by the American Society for the Prevention of Cruelty to Animals, the total estimated cost for the first year of owning a large breed dog, such as a Labrador Retriever, is $1,500. This estimate covers exams, vaccinations, heartworm preventative, spay/neuter expense, food, toys and other incidentals, but does not include training.

"Wet puppy kisses and happy tail wags come with no additional expense," he concludes.

MIXED-BREEDS ARE SMART, TOO

It's time for mixed-breed dogs to step to the front of the line, show their intelligence and have some fun.

The American Kennel Club, the world's largest purebred canine registry, recently announced the creation of a new program for these wonderful animals, many of which have been adopted from animal shelters and city pounds.

As of October 1, 2009 owners of mixed breed dogs and hybrids, such as Labradoodles, can begin enrolling their four-footed friends and receive an AKC identification number. Beginning next April 1, enrolled dogs will be eligible to compete in mixed-breed classes at stand-alone AKC agility, obedience and rally events. These competitions will not be part of regular AKC licensed events held for purebred dogs.

Other benefits include discounted participation in the AKC Companion Animal Recovery Lost and Found service, a free AKC Canine Good Citizen certificate for dogs passing the C.G.C. test, a free initial veterinary visit, a trial offer for pet insurance and numerous discount coupons for pet supplies.

The third phase of the new program will offer a dedicated website where dog owners can interact via an online community with discussion forums and access dog care video downloads, advice from experts and the most up-to-date news on canine health and welfare. The site will continually be enhanced with new features and benefits in order to respond to the changing needs of pet owners.

The AKC hopes that the new program will not only improve the lives of hundreds of thousands of mixed-breed dogs, but will also help local kennel clubs attract new members and educate more dog owners. The new development will enable the organization to broaden its legislative influence at all levels of government by representing more dog owners and will further promote responsible dog ownership.

According to Gail Zurawski, obedience coordinator for the Wampanoag Kennel Club in New Bedford, Massachusetts, separate competitions for mixed-breeds is a good idea. She adds that these dogs have always been welcomed in obedience classes offered by the club.

"We have quite a few that come for training," she begins, adding that owners are more likely to relinquish a mixed-breed that constantly misbehaves faster than they would a purebred canine that cost a lot of money.

Zurawski has seen many unusual crosses during the 15 years that she has served as obedience coordinator, including a "Boogle" — a Beagle-Boxer mix that recently completed a basic obedience class. The kennel club offers obedience instruction from beginning to advanced classes on Wednesday nights that are attended by dog owners from all over the area.

The longtime obedience enthusiast recalls that she owned several mixed-breed dogs before purchasing a Cocker Spaniel many years ago. Several of Zurawski's dogs have earned obedience degrees and Canine Good Citizen titles and regularly visit local nursing homes.

She hopes that more owners of mixed-breed dogs will participate in the new AKC program and become involved in the sport of dogs. Zurawski emphasizes that the activities that will be offered for mixed-breed dogs are ideal for families, and teach children about good sportsmanship and responsibility.

"A lot of people can't afford a purebred dog," Zurawski notes, adding that many folks also prefer to adopt a homeless dog from a shelter to give the animal a second chance of having a good life.

Zurawski says that the current AKC rules that allow spayed or neutered dogs to participate in performance activities such as obedience, rally and agility will apply to mixed-breed dogs. Altered canines cannot compete in conformation events.

"You'll have a much better dog all around if its spayed or neutered," she believes.

Zurawski notes that the Wampanoag Kennel Club officials will study the new mixed-breed program and if there is sufficient local interest, will conduct separate obedience trials for these dogs. Although the club currently does not offer agility, dog owners interested in that activity can be referred to clubs in the area.

For more information, call the Wampanoag Kennel Club at (508) 673-3066.

VERSATILE GERMAN SHEPHERD IS ADMIRED THROUGHOUT THE WORLD

The iconic German Shepherd Dog is one of world's more easily recognized, popular and versatile breeds.

Known for its keen intelligence and loyalty, this noble herding dog has excelled for more than 100 years as a guide for the sight-impaired, aided law enforcement in a variety of capacities, assisted farmers by keeping flocks together and served as a beloved family pet and protector.

The breed, which was developed in the late 1800s by farmers from indigenous farming stock to herd sheep and protect flocks from predators, ranked second in the number of registrations for 2012 according to the American Kennel Club. It was the fourth consecutive year that the athletic herding dog captured that position on the AKC's top ten list, falling behind the Labrador Retriever.

Surprisingly, the German Shepherd is a relatively new breed when compared to other herding breeds, such as the Pembroke Welsh Corgi, whose lineage can be traced for several hundred years.

America's great interest in the German Shepherd blossomed shortly after World War I when Rin Tin Tin, a rescued war dog, appeared on the silver screen. The canine was an immediate box office success and was followed by a succession of similar dogs all bearing the same moniker whose fearlessness captured the attention of the young and old alike for decades, first in movies and later on television.

Some readers may remember the popular TV children's series *The Adventures of Rin Tin Tin*, which aired in the late 1950s, featuring an orphaned young boy and his dog who were adopted by soldiers in the United States Cavalry, and who subsequently helped the officers keep law and order in the Wild West.

As young American families moved to suburbia in the late 1950s and early 1960s, the German Shepherd became a popular family pet. New owners quickly appreciated the breed's keen intelligence and noble character.

Fairhaven, Massachusetts resident Susan Amaral has been a fan of German Shepherds for 50 years. Her lifelong interest in the breed began when her parents Conrad and Shirley Richard of nearby Acushnet purchased a hardy dog named Sam to protect their three young daughters. Amaral's aunt, Barbara Plant of Dartmouth, a respected breeder of champion Norwegian Elkhounds, recommended the herding breed as a worthy protector.

"I think he is the reason I continue to love the shepherd," Amaral, now age 58, begins. "It was his loyalty and his protection."

Amaral says Sam lived for 14 years and inspired her to own these dogs for most of her adult life. She admits that her husband Keith and children Valerie and Bradley also have acquired a love for the handsome breed.

The longtime dog fanciers currently share their home with Jazz, a 10-year-old spayed female, and Uno, a neutered 10-month-old male, who recently started training to compete in rally exercises.

Uno was bred by local veterinarian Dr. Christine Gaumont, owner of Acushnet Animal Hospital, and a respected longtime breeder of German Shepherds.

"He's the most incredible German Shepherd that we've ever owned," Amaral says, adding that the handsome black and red-colored dog has a luxurious coat and a "solid temperament" that makes Uno a pleasure to own.

"Not much bothers him," the dog's owner adds, noting that these canines make "excellent companions."

Amaral urges potential shepherd owners to talk to knowledgeable breeders who screen for health issues and breed animals with sound temperaments.

According to the American Kennel Club, a German Shepherd should present an impression of a strong, agile, well-muscled animal that is confident, alert and full of life. Dogs that are either shy or aggressive should be disqualified from the ring at competitions.

Amaral emphasizes that these powerful, medium sized dogs need to be taught manners.

"Training a German Shepherd is a job," she admits, adding that Gaumont starts teaching her young puppies basic manners before they are sold to their new homes.

"If you don't start it when they are young, a German Shepherd will train you," Amaral warns.

As Uno matures, the dog continues obedience training under the guidance of John Soule, owner of Battleship K-9 in Fall River, Massachusetts, a German Shepherd breeder and obedience instructor with more than four decades of experience.

"I love him," Soule says of his prized canine pupil. "Uno is what a shepherd should be."

The training instructor also emphasizes that shepherds, like all dogs, need structure.

"They are working dogs and they need training to work seamlessly with their owner," he says. "The dogs look for direction; they accept it willingly and perform it willingly."

Several years ago, Amaral wove her interest in dogs and skills as a potter together to design dog bone and paw print ornaments that she creates in her home studio.

"I always work with a German Shepherd at my feet," she says.

OUTDOOR POOLS BRING JOY, STIMULATE CONVERSATION

If you've always been fascinated by dazzling goldfish and other swimming creatures, late spring is the perfect time to install an outdoor pond.

Marine animal expert and tropical fish hobbyist Richard Rego says that fishponds can range from a plastic container the size of a litter box to large professionally designed structures with waterfalls and other enhancements.

"Ponds are pretty to look at and people enjoy watching fish," the Swansea, Massachusetts resident says. "It's another form of gardening, too."

Rego says that unless an owner plans to remove fish once temperatures drop to 32° or below and bring the creatures indoors, the pond or container must be at least three feet deep to allow the fish to live under the ice once the water freezes.

"The fish left outdoors stop feeding in late fall and go into a dormant state," Rego says, adding that outdoor ponds must have either a waterfall or electrically powered floating deicer that will create an opening in the frozen pond.

"A hole in the ice allows a gas exchange: carbon dioxide is released and oxygen flows in to keep the fish alive," he says.

Rego says that goldfish, carp and Koi, a colorful fish native to Japan, are among the most popular varieties of pond fish. Other varieties include Golden Orfe and Tench fish.

"All of these are cold tolerant that can survive in our area," Rego says.

According to the marine animal expert, wild fish normally stock up — somewhat like squirrels — during the summer months and build up enough fat to survive through the winter when they get little or no food while dormant. Rego adds that when water temperatures dip below 50°, fish cannot digest their food.

"Once the warmer weather arrives, the first inclination that fish have is to breed and then they eat to put on weight for the next winter," he says. "If the fish are healthy going into the winter months, they should survive."

According to Rego, all fishponds require regular maintenance, which varies according to the size of the pool. Rain does help replenish water that has evaporated, but owners must check water levels, remove algae and feed the fish.

Rego warns that owners should be prepared to pay additional electrical costs incurred by fountains, waterfalls, deicers and lights. Surprisingly, he adds that although fishponds are often installed to enhance property, they can also be a detriment because many prospective homebuyers don't want to deal with the responsibilities and costs of maintaining a pond.

The respected aquaculturist advises pond owners not to introduce native wildlife — such as frogs, turtles and fish found in local waters — into backyard habitats.

"You run the risk of introducing disease and parasites," he warns, adding, "Frogs won't stay where they are replanted." Sometimes however, he notes, inquisitive amphibians will discover and relocate in the new habitat.

Rego notes that to enhance the beauty of a pond, owners can place cultivated lilies and other water plants that can be purchased from a garden center whose staff are knowledgeable about creating these colorful habitats.

He warns pond owners never to release excess Koi and other fish into the wild because they become easy prey for waterfowl, storks and osprey.

"The biggest pests are Great Blue Herons," Rego says. "They are notorious for finding Koi ponds and wiping them out in a few days. For them, it's like an all-you-can-eat buffet."

To protect fish, he recommends placing a protective net over the pond to ward off predators.

Once temperatures rise, fishponds run the risk of becoming mosquito breeding grounds. To avoid this problem, Rego suggests using biological insecticides to control pests, and purchasing a test kit to keep track of water quality.

He also recommends that pond owners with small children and young pets install short fences around the pools to prevent accidents.

"Read books and magazines, visit garden centers, get some design ideas, learn about fish and have a lot of fun," Rego suggests.

NORWEGIAN FOREST CAT BRINGS JOY TO OWNERS

Bugsy is one of the luckiest and most handsome tomcats in all of Southern New England.

The hefty three-year-old Norwegian Forest cat is the prized companion of Somerset, Massachusetts residents Roxanne and Paul Winsor, two devoted cat fanciers who have turned the feline's life around by showering the once-abandoned animal with lots of love and affection.

The Winsors discovered the large black and white cat two years ago, sitting in a cage at a Rhode Island pet expo. Officials of the shelter that was providing temporary care for the charming cat had their fingers crossed, hoping that one of the thousands of animal-loving spectators who attended the event would open their heart and hearth to the homeless creature.

According to Roxanne, the longtime cat lovers had been searching for several months to find a buddy for Pashi, the couple's elderly Persian cat that became depressed and lethargic after their other cat died.

"We got him on Valentine's Day," she continues, recalling that once the couple spotted Bugsy, they immediately knew they had found the perfect match.

"He was lying in a litter box," Paul remembers. "He took up most of it."

When the Winsors inquired about the cat, they were told that Bugsy, then named Sylvester, suffered from asthma and other ailments and that the feline was relinquished because the tomcat's previous owner couldn't afford the cost of long-term veterinary care.

The Norwegian Forest cat breed standard reveals that these hardy, friendly cats were once used by the Vikings to rid ships and coastal villages of vermin. The breed is known for its strong, sturdy body and thick, water-repellant coat, which helps the personable feline endure the Scandinavian Peninsula's harsh climate.

Historians report that by the 20th century, these cats faced extinction. World War II interrupted the work of some Scandinavian fanciers who tried to renew interest in the breed, and finally, about 40 years ago, a few Norsemen developed a special breeding program to help protect these photogenic felines. The breeders' efforts were bolstered when the late King Olaf V designated the Norwegian Forest cat as the official cat of its picturesque homeland.

These cats have an affectionate personality, but some specimens have a genetic predisposition to kidney and heart conditions. Bugsy, in addition to suffering from occasional urinary tract infections, also has periodic asthma attacks.

To better control these medical issues, the Winsors feed the 17-pound tomcat a grain-free diet and small pieces of diced raw chicken. The cat is treated by a homeopathic veterinarian who prescribes natural remedies, and occasionally conventional medication to restore the animal's health.

"He does demand to eat frequently," Roxanne admits, noting that the cat's name was changed to reflect the fact that he was always "bugging" the couple for food.

The Winsors monitor the cat's weight every two weeks to prevent the feline from becoming overweight and developing additional medical problems, such as diabetes and arthritis.

In addition to having a fluffy tail and a luxurious coat, the Norwegian Forest cat is also known for its engaging personality and strong desire to be part of the family.

"Bugsy wears his heart on his sleeve," Roxanne says, adding that he expresses his needs and desires through body language.

"His eyes are the window to his soul," she continues. "They express a variety of emotions from love to hurt and disappointment when he doesn't get his own way."

The compassionate cat owner reveals that Bugsy expresses contentment by purring and kneading his paws.

"He rolls around and looks up at you when he wants attention," she says, laughing. "Norwegian Forest cats are intelligent and very affectionate."

Roxanne adds that although veterinary care can be expensive, she urges potential owners never to hesitate adopting a feline that has special requirements.

"These cats will thank you a million times over," she emphasizes. "You have to be devoted, have patience, and have an intuitive sense of how to treat the animal holistically — looking at the cat as a whole."

The longtime feline fancier says caring for a cat with chronic medical conditions is similar to treating an elderly relative.

"God doesn't make mistakes," she concludes. "Don't turn away from a cat that has special needs."

WATCH OUT: COYOTES ARE ON THE PROWL

Wildlife experts emphasize that it's important for pet owners to protect domesticated animals from being killed or severely maimed by prowling coyotes searching for food.

"Coyotes are a very successful species," begins Bill Sampson, head zookeeper at Buttonwood Park Zoo in New Bedford, Massachusetts.

"They are extremely opportunistic," he continues. "They will eat anything — plant or animal."

Sampson has gained a wealth of knowledge by caring for the zoo's two male coyotes, a lanky, long-legged Eastern Coyote that resembles a young German Shepherd, and a shorter, much heavier Western Coyote that looks like a fox.

"A coyote is just another example of a wild dog," Sampson notes. "They are probably smarter than the average domesticated dog."

The experienced zookeeper says that when a coyote comes out of hiding and stalks, its brain is telling the animal that it needs food.

"They will eat anything that's available," Sampson discloses, adding that coyotes are omnivores. "They will dig up onions and even earthworms."

Wildlife experts recall that the Eastern Coyote first appeared in Massachusetts during the 1950s and now inhabits every part of the state, except for Nantucket and Martha's Vineyard.

Coyotes primarily eat fruit, berries, some vegetables, small rodents, rabbits, birds, snakes, frogs and a variety of insects. These predators scavenge on animal remains, including road-kill, garbage and pet food left outdoors. Unprotected pets, such as outdoor cats and unsupervised dogs, are also sources of food.

Wildlife experts emphasize that because coyotes utilize so many food sources, these feral animals have adapted to and live in a variety of habitats, including urban and heavily populated suburban areas. For example, Sampson reports that a young female coyote lives in the neighborhood adjacent to the zoo and hunts on the park's grounds every morning.

"They've learned to live near people," Sampson reveals, adding that coyotes hunt individually, in pairs or in family packs that consist of two parents and their pups.

Experts say that although most coyotes are shy and prefer to hunt nocturnally, some are less apprehensive and show little fear of humans. Sampson says it's important for folks who encounter a coyote to stand their ground and not let the stalking creature gain control of the situation.

"Coyotes are territorial," Sampson emphasizes. "If you claim your territory, they won't stay around. He adds that the marauding predators can be thwarted by banging pots, shouting, being struck by a rock or tennis ball or doused with a garden hose. At night, dog walkers should always carry a flashlight to scare off any stalking predator.

"Never leave pets outdoors," he warns, adding that pet food dishes also attract coyotes, as well as other wildlife species foraging for food. Experts reveal that coyotes, like dogs, can climb short fences, which should be protected with barbed wire to prevent invaders from gaining access to loose pets relaxing in a fenced-in yard.

Coyotes are also able to dig, and poorly secured fences provide an open invitation for these curious creatures. Sampson says that a coyote is persistent, and will keep returning to a site — if not challenged by a human — until it can wield its way under the fence and gain access to prey.

Sampson urges folks with bird feeders to keep the area underneath the receptacle clean because small rodents eat the seeds and become easy targets for wandering coyotes.

"It's the same for fruit trees," he adds, noting that coyotes like to snack on fallen apples, pears, peaches and other fruits.

Sampson and wildlife experts agree that coyotes have their place in the animal hierarchy and benefit society by controlling rodent populations. He adds that although all mammals can contract rabies, skunks and raccoons are more likely to become infected.

"No one should ever go near any wildlife," he urges, adding that children should be taught not to approach coyote pups, which often appear in late spring and can be confused with mixed-breed domesticated puppies. Coyote pups are cute, but they are also dangerous.

"I wouldn't encourage anyone to get between a coyote and another animal," Sampson warns, adding that if an owner can successfully release a cat or dog that has been attacked, the wounded animal should be rushed to an emergency veterinary clinic for treatment. Humans who have physical contact with a coyote should report immediately to an emergency room.

Dartmouth, Massachusetts farmer and part-time Animal Control Officer Cheryl Jackson reports that she hasn't had any problems with coyotes on her farm. She raises goats and sheep and owns a llama.

"I haven't seen one on my farm," she reports. "I've never heard one howling."

Jackson, however, acknowledges that the animal control office does receive occasional telephone calls from residents who've spotted a coyote wandering in the area.

One dog, a Labrador Retriever, was attacked by a coyote in Dartmouth last August and recovered; and there have been recent published reports of farmers in the town who have had livestock killed by coyotes but who did not notify authorities.

PHOTOGRAPHER CAPTURES BEAUTY OF NEWBORN PUPPIES

Anyone who has ever raised a litter of puppies knows what an incredible experience it is to watch the tiny creatures navigate from their mother's side to the outside world.

The first three weeks of a dog's life are critical as the creature grows, opens its eyes and ears, and becomes familiar with its surroundings and human family. Many times, much to a breeder's dismay, a newborn puppy born with birth defects can die or even a healthy puppy can be crushed by its mother's weight.

Celebrated Rhode Island author and photographer Traer Scott has captured this magical time in a canine's journey in a charming new coffee table book entitled *Newborn Puppies: Dogs in Their First Three Weeks* (Chronicle Books, 2013) that captures the delicate beauty of young purebred and shelter puppies photographed during the first days of their young lives.

"It was a fun project," Scott begins, adding that she visited hobby breeders and animal shelters in Massachusetts, Connecticut and Rhode Island to photograph the adorable pups.

The lifelong animal lover and advocate reveals that the book sends readers a "strong anti-puppy mill message" and urges people not to purchase canines from large commercial breeders. She recommends buying from reputable hobby kennels or visiting local shelters that often care for abandoned nursing mothers and their young offspring.

Scott tells that her great love for dogs began as a young child growing up in the South. Her family owned Cocker Spaniels, and she's also owned several mixed-breeds, including her current canine companion, a Pitbull-mix. As a child, she enjoyed attending

97

dog shows and agility trials, where she learned about various breeds and witnessed the unbreakable bond that develops between a dog and its handler.

After graduating from North Carolina State University and the New England School of Photography in the late 1990s, Scott settled in Providence, where she had spent a college summer internship working at Brown University.

"I really loved Providence so I moved here," she says. Although she enjoys being "behind the lens" and also offers customized portrait commissions of people — usually with the creatures that they love — Scott's real passion is capturing the irresistible beauty and quirky sense of humor of man's best friend.

"I love dogs," the artist emphasizes. "Dogs are one of my favorite things in the whole world." In addition to canines, the photographer also likes spending time with her husband and new daughter.

One of Scott's most popular books is *Shelter Dogs* (Merrell, 2006), which features 50 soulful portraits of abandoned canines patiently waiting for new and loving homes. The inspiration for the collection came from the photographer's volunteer work at the Providence Animal Shelter. Many of the portraits were taken at local pounds.

In addition to the beautiful photographs, Scott also informs readers about each shelter dog's fate. Although many of the canines were successfully adopted into loving homes, some, sadly, were euthanized.

"The book advocates for adoption and volunteerism," Scott emphasizes, adding that people can help homeless animals in many ways, including fundraising, donating supplies and assisting at adoption events. For folks who have the time and energy, there's always plenty of work to be done at a shelter, including bathing, grooming and feeding animals, doing laundry and walking dogs.

With her attention still focused on the plight of homeless canines, Scott subsequently published *Street Dogs* (Merrell 2007), a fascinating collection of photos of hounds found living on the streets in Mexico and Puerto Rico.

Noting that there are now more than 200,000 feral dogs inhabiting the streets of the Caribbean island, Scott adds that those animals "face a short, brutal life."

The goals of the book, she reveals, are to heighten awareness of the existence of those animals and to encourage Americans to help in rescue efforts. During the past few years, many healthy canines have been adopted by visiting tourists or shipped to shelters on the mainland to be adopted by new loving owners.

In addition to the dog books, Scott also attracted widespread attention with her book *Wild Horses: Engaged Beauty* (Merrell 2008) in which she expertly captures the magnificence of America's wild equines, whose population is decreasing as a result of encroachment and government-ordered roundups.

Scott traveled throughout the Western states and to the Vieques National Wildlife Refuge in Puerto Rico to photograph the horses.

Some publishers have asked Scott to submit a cat book, but she says that won't happen. "I'm allergic to cats," she says, laughing. "I can't even touch them."

Scott's books can be ordered online from Amazon or purchased at local bookstores.

LET'S KEEP THOSE NEW YEAR'S RESOLUTIONS

Happy New Year!

When we turn the page on the calendar and start a new year, most of us make a few resolutions that unfortunately are forgotten by the end of January.

This time, let's all vow to improve our lives and those of our pets by making permanent lifestyle changes, such as losing weight, eating healthier foods, getting lots of exercise and maintaining regular medical and veterinary appointments.

According to Chicago-based pet expert Steve Dale, pet owners can do a better job of providing preventative care for their faithful family companions.

"Our pets deserve better," the acclaimed author, radio and TV personality begins, adding that despite the fact that more than half of American households own a pet and most pet owners consider Rover or Kitty to be part of the family, veterinary visits — especially those for preventative care — are on the decline.

"As a result, pets and pet owners are paying a significant price," Dale emphasizes. "My resolution for 2013 will be to play whatever role I can in reversing this alarming trend. The decline in veterinary visits is entirely contradictory to what is in the best interest of our pets."

The *USA Weekend* columnist cites the 2011 Banfield Pet Hospital Report on pet health, which states that many preventable medical problems, including flea infestations and heartworm disease, are on the rise.

"Flea infestations and heartworm are far more expensive to treat than to prevent, which is always the case; prevention is less expensive," Dale continues, adding that when precautions are taken, both problems can easily be avoided.

He notes that veterinarians continue to report an increase of pets suffering from flea allergies, and adds that although heartworm can be fatal, the regimen of treatments required to combat the disease can be grueling for a pet.

"Obviously pets don't get to vote. They clearly would choose prevention rather than crazily itching from flea allergies or suffering the effects of heartworm," Dale remarks, noting that early detection can also save pets from certain forms of cancer, heart and kidney disease. When an owner detects an abnormality in the pet's physical condition or changes in the animal's behavior, the pet should be brought to the veterinarian immediately so that any medical problems can be diagnosed and effectively treated.

Fall River, Massachusetts resident and Borzoi fancier Winnie Kelly agrees with Dale and reveals that one of her New Year's resolutions is to monitor her senior cats' and dogs' health more closely "in order to catch health problems early on."

According to Kelly, painful conditions such as arthritis can be prevented from worsening if owners are proactive and develop a treatment plan with their veterinarian.

"If you nip the problem in the bud, it will cost you less money and fewer trips to the vet," Kelly emphasizes.

The lifelong animal lover also agrees with Dale that cat owners, especially those with senior cats, have to be especially observant since felines often mask health issues that exacerbate over time. For example, it a feline is drinking excessive amounts of water, the animal may be suffering from kidney disease or diabetes.

Kelly says another resolution she's made is to watch her senior pets' weight more closely and place some of the animals on a specially formulated diet. Overweight pets, like their human counterparts, often develop heart conditions and orthopedic issues that can seriously affect the animal's health if left untreated.

Another New Year's resolution that Kelly has made is to purchase an extra bag of dry dog or cat food or a bag of kitty litter when she's at the supermarket and donate it to a local animal shelter. These facilities also need towels, disinfectant, laundry detergent, paper towels and pet toys, and they always welcome any monetary donation.

Fairhaven, Massachusetts resident and Toy Fox Terrier breeder Samantha Gershman reports her New Year's resolutions include trimming her dogs' nails every weekend, and allowing her oldest dog to sleep on the bed at night.

"I also resolve to spend more couch time with all of my dogs, despite their occasional squabbling," she says, laughing.

AM STAFFS ARE OFTEN WRONGFULLY MALIGNED

One breed that has always been a standout in the terrier group is the handsome American Staffordshire Terrier, a breed that is often maligned because of the actions of a few of its poorly trained canine cousins and their irresponsible owners.

Despite the negativity that sometimes surrounds the breed when it gets confused with other dogs, dedicated Am Staff fanciers, such as Monique Bertrand, owner of TradeWind Kennels in New Bedford, Massachusetts, continue to breed and exhibit quality animals with sound temperaments that make good family pets.

Bertrand became interested in the breed in 2001, and spent several months conducting research to determine whether the Am Staff would be a good choice for her lifestyle.

"I went to dog shows and met people," she says. "I wanted to get into showing, and it became so much more."

In the past 12 years, Bertrand, who once exhibited Morgan horses, has assisted in writing generic, non-breed specific dog ordinances in several communities throughout Massachusetts, and successfully handled four dogs to AKC championships.

Bertrand's dogs also compete in performance activities, including obedience and rally exercises.

Her current star is Ch. TradeWind's Talisman, who has also earned Rally Novice, Canine Good Citizen (C.G.C.) and Temperament Tested (T.T.) titles.

"Their loyalty, courage, and loving companionship make them the wonderful breed they are," Bertrand adds. "These are truly companion dogs, who thrive on human interaction and attention."

Breed historians believe that the ancestors of the modern Am Staff were developed in 19th century England by crossing the Bulldog with one or more terrier varieties. The Staffordshire Terrier was introduced to America in the 1870s, and accepted by the AKC in 1936. Subsequently, some American fanciers developed a heavier canine, and in 1972, the breed's name was changed to distinguish it from its smaller relative, which is still called the Staffordshire Terrier.

According to the breed standard, the Am Staff should always give the impression of great strength for its size and must always be keenly aware of its surroundings. Although stocky and muscular, these dogs should be agile and graceful, but should never be long-legged and racy in outline like a Whippet.

Bertrand, who has bred one litter, emphasizes that producing healthy dogs with a sound temperament is most important, as well as maintaining proper structure and type, which can be defined as the sum of qualities that distinguish one breed from another.

"A well-bred Am Staff should always have an outgoing and friendly nature and should never be timid or shy, especially toward humans," Bertrand explains, adding that the breed can display some level of dog aggression, the amount depending on the individual dog. Each canine has a unique personality and responds to situations in different ways.

She adds that although potential owners should understand and accept this trait, dog aggression should never be confused with human aggression, which never should be tolerated.

"My dogs get along but I am the boss," Bertrand says, adding that her canines are separated when she is not at home to avoid any concerns.

The Am Staff fancier says that proper socialization, discipline and consistent ongoing training are key to owning a well-behaved specimen of the breed.

"They are great with children, and will watch over their home and family," she continues, explaining that although the Am Staff, as is the case of every terrier, can be tenacious and stubborn, they can also be "playful clowns" that, when properly socialized, are loyal and loving family companions.

"One must realize that when looking for a dog to be part of your family, the Am Staff is not a breed for everyone, and you must have an understanding of the breed and accept the responsibility of owning one," Bertrand adds.

Although the Am Staff is capable of performing many roles, including serving as a therapy dog, these canines should not be used as guard dogs and placed in situations that are contrary to their nature as dogs that thrive on positive human interaction. Bertrand says that many of the Pitbulls that cause harm are mixed-breeds that are improperly trained.

"A well-bred American Pitbull Terrier should have the same character and traits as the Am Staff," Bertrand says.

WHAT'S GOING ON IN YOUR PET'S MOUTH?

Imagine what your mouth would look and feel like if you went for several years without brushing your teeth or visiting the dentist.

Your mouth would not be too healthy.

Just like their masters, pets also need regular dental care.

"Many owners don't realize this, but dental disease is actually the most common disease we see in dogs and cats," begins Dr. Michelle Zarif of Veterinary Associates of Cape Cod in Yarmouth, Massachusetts.

The small-animal practitioner reports that studies have shown that more than 80 percent of all cats and dogs age 3 and older suffer from dental disease. The progressive condition, if not treated properly, can cause additional serious medical problems.

According to Zarif, dental disease starts with plaque buildup on the surface of the teeth. When plaque is hardened by chemicals in the animal's saliva, it forms tartar, which accumulates under the gum line and can lead to gingivitis, an infection of the gums.

The respected veterinarian adds that without medical intervention, the painful condition causes gums to recede, and sensitive tooth roots and underlying bone become exposed and infected.

"Once bone loss begins, it is an irreversible process," Zarif continues. "The good news is that gingivitis is a preventable and reversible process. Early intervention is the key to stopping the progression of this common ailment."

Zarif, a graduate of Tufts University Cummings School of Veterinary Medicine, urges owners to be observant and proactive, and emphasizes that tartar buildup can be prevented with regular dental care.

"Although regular brushing is by far the best way to prevent tartar buildup, there are many products designed to help prevent tartar from accumulating," Zarif says, adding that some chew toys and specially formulated dental diets can also help combat dental disease.

Pet writer and author Amy Shojai reveals, "Feeding pets foods that have some 'detergent' action can help.

"Dry foods only help about 10 percent, and canned/moist diets really may cause problems," she says. Shojai recommends offering pets treats that encourage chewing and/or contain chlorhexidine and zinc ascorbate, which kill the bacteria that cause periodontal disease.

"Rawhide chews, dental hygiene chew toys, and treats like Greenies work well," she continues. "Some dogs enjoy fresh carrots and apple slices. Cats benefit from a chunk of firm steak now and then that they must chew."

Zarif notes that sometimes tartar must be professionally removed and teeth surfaces must be polished and disinfected.

"This procedure is very similar to what you and I receive at our dentist's office," the veterinarian reveals. "The only difference is that our patients require anesthesia to properly perform a successful oral examination and cleaning and scaling both above and below the gum line."

She urges owners to implement a preventative dental plan early in a pet's life.

"Puppies and kittens should become used to having their mouth touched and teeth examined from a young age," the veterinarian says, adding that owners must be careful to use specially formulated enzymatic toothpaste available in "pet friendly flavors" such as beef and poultry for dogs, and seafood for cats.

"Although a small human toothbrush may be used, human toothpaste should never be used in pets," Zarif warns.

Shojai recommends squirting a small amount of doggie toothpaste on a canine's favorite chew toy or allowing a kitten to lick a dab of feline toothpaste from its owner's fingertip.

According to Zarif, it's important for owners to examine their pet's mouth because few critters show signs of dental disease until the condition becomes more advanced.

"Early signs of dental disease include bad breath and red, irritated gums," she reveals. "Pets with advanced dental disease may be reluctant to eat, drop food from their mouth, paw at their face or drool excessively."

The small-animal expert says that as dental disease progresses, gum infections can spread to bones and sinuses.

"If bone infection is severe enough, this can actually cause the jaw to break," Zarif reveals. "Even worse than that, bacteria can be absorbed into the bloodstream and carried to other organs, such as the heart, liver, and kidneys. Heart valve infections (also known as endocardiosis or endocarditis) are frequently caused by dental disease."

She notes that surgical removal is necessary when dental disease "has been allowed to progress to a point where the tooth is no longer salvageable.

"I never remove a tooth unless it is absolutely necessary," Zarif informs. "My goal is to intervene before the dental disease progresses to this point, when the process is still reversible and the tooth can be saved."

IRISH RED AND WHITE — A UNIQUE SETTER

If you go to a dog show this year, chances are you might see an Irish Red and White Setter, the newest member of the sporting group. The centuries old hunting breed became eligible to compete at AKC events on January 1, 2009.

Debbie Cournoyer, corresponding secretary of the Irish Red and White Setter Association, the breed's parent club, reports there are about 600 of these sporting dogs registered in the foundation stock studbook in the United States. She believes there might also be a few more specimens scattered across the country whose owners haven't registered their dogs and just keep them as pets or use the canines to hunt.

Cournoyer, a resident of West Kingston, Rhode Island, owns five of these setters and hopes to have a few champions by the end of the year, now that the breed can be exhibited at AKC licensed events. The experienced handler is a longtime Gordon Setter fancier and exhibitor, and acquired her first Irish Red and White Setter in 2000.

"They are unique and very pretty, " Cournoyer begins. "These dogs are highly intelligent and creative. They like to solve problems, real or imagined."

To an untrained eye, the Irish Red and White Setter might first appear to be a mixed-breed. Unlike its cousins — the Irish, Gordon and English Setters — the Irish Red and White doesn't have a racy outline and is not excessively trimmed. The breed standard advises judges to evaluate these dogs primarily from a working standpoint.

Breed historians report that the Irish Red and White Setter was developed by Irish sportsmen in the late 17th century and most likely is the progenitor of the more popular Irish Setter, known in Ireland and much of Europe simply as the "red setter."

By the late 19th century, the red setter had eclipsed its bi-colored ancestor in popularity, and the Irish Red and White almost became extinct.

Although the energetic and aristocratic Irish Setter has always been a beloved family pet in this country, Cournoyer attributes the breed's surge in popularity in the early 1960s to the blockbuster movie *Big Red*, a heartwarming tale set in Canada about the adventures of a heroic Irish Setter.

Meanwhile, the Irish Red and White Setter languished in obscurity.

In the mid-1970s, a handful of the dog fanciers in Ireland and this country became concerned about the breed's demise and developed well-planned breeding programs. Many sportsmen prized the dogs for their versatility and keen hunting ability, and breeding stock was soon exported to many parts of the world.

Today, the Irish Red and White Setter can be found throughout the British Isles, as well as in Belgium, Italy, Scandinavia and Canada. Cournoyer reports that there is also great interest in the breed in several South American countries, including Brazil and Argentina.

The dedicated breed enthusiast says that one of the highlights of her involvement with this intelligent breed has been attending two international conferences and specialty shows where she met fellow hobbyists from all over the world. Cournoyer traveled to Belgium in 2004 and to Ireland in 2006.

Unlike the Gordon Setter, which tries constantly to please its owner, Cournoyer reveals that the Irish Red and White, like many Irishmen, has an independent streak.

"They can accomplish a task by themselves, whereas the Gordon seeks direction and wants to please," she observes. She adds that an Irish Red and White Setter will work well with its owner once the pair develops a solid relationship.

"There has to be some camaraderie," she continues.

Cournoyer hopes that the Irish Red and White Setter will become more widely accepted now that it's officially recognized by the AKC.

"Their sheer beauty will absolutely get your attention," she says. "Your eye is drawn to them."

The dog lover says she was attracted to the noble hunting breed by its shimmering white coat, which Cournoyer describes as "pearlescent" and the rich mahogany-colored markings or large spots that the breed standard refers to as "islands."

Another physical trait that caught the dog lover's eye is the long, flowing, silky hair, known as "feathers," that appear on the legs, tail and ears.

"The feathers are the icing on the cake," she concludes.

SUMMER CAN BE DANGEROUS FOR PETS

Veterinarians warn that the "dog days of summer" can be a dangerous time for our companion animals.

They urge owners to take a few minutes to carefully plan and monitor their pet's outdoor activities and safeguard cats and dogs against suffering heat stroke, a serious health issue that can lead to death if not promptly treated by medical personnel.

According to Dr. Tom Burns of Veterinary Associates of Cape Cod in South Yarmouth, Massachusetts, the most common cause of heat stroke in dogs is leaving the animal in a hot car with poor ventilation.

"Many dog owners do not realize that even with the windows open and water in the car, the temperature still can quickly become deadly on a summer day," Burns begins. "Dogs cannot sweat beyond their feet to regulate body heat, and their main means of cooling is by panting."

Dogs that are muzzled are at much more risk of heat stroke since they cannot pant to cool themselves and sometimes suffer an untimely death.

The veterinarian emphasizes that since the airflow in a parked car is insufficient, the body temperature of a canine left in such a vehicle can elevate within minutes. If the dog becomes anxious or starts barking, its situation only worsens.

"I suspect that dying of heat stroke in a parked car would be one of the worst ways for a dog to die," Burns comments.

Signs of heat stroke include heavy panting, salivation, lethargy, vomiting and diarrhea, and if not promptly treated, seizures and death.

"Safe reduction of body temperature is the goal," Burns continues, adding that after consulting with a veterinarian, an owner can douse the overheated dog with water, or apply wet towels to the canine's head, stomach, underarms, back and legs.

Pets should always be offered an ample bowl of cool, fresh water. Owners should quickly remove bowls of uneaten food, which can quickly spoil in the heat and cause gastric problems.

If the dog's body temperature was not elevated for an extended period of time and the animal is otherwise healthy, Burns says the prognosis for the canine's recovery is often good. However, if a dog survives a sustained period of heat stroke, organ damage and subsequent failure may occur, sometimes resulting in premature death.

"My first recommendation is to try to avoid peak sun time if at all possible," the veterinarian notes, adding that direct sunlight, especially when dogs are left in a yard without shade, can be deadly. In the summer, it's safer to walk dogs at dawn or dusk and only let them outside for a few minutes during the day to go to the bathroom.

Burns says owners can use regular sunscreen with a high sun protection factor (S.P.F.) but it shouldn't contain zinc, which is toxic to dogs. Sunscreen can also be used in small amounts on cat ear tips, one of the most common areas where skin cancers develop in light-coated outdoor felines.

The small-animal practitioner reports that overexertion in warm weather is another leading cause of heat stroke in dogs. Canines that are overweight, or members of a bracycephalic (short nosed) breed such as Boxers, Pugs, Bulldogs, Boston Terriers or French Bulldogs are highly susceptible.

"In those breeds, and in just excessively exercised or excited dogs, heat stroke can occur when it does not seem that hot or humid," Burns discloses.

Although it's important that man's best friend doesn't become overexerted when temperatures soar, all pets need some form of exercise throughout the year. Burns notes that cool dips in a pond or river can be a nice way to get a little activity while cooling off.

"It's also a great low-impact exercise for overweight or arthritic pets," he adds, emphasizing that short swims should always be supervised by someone who has the ability to take action if the dog suddenly becomes ill or distressed.

Burns also urges dog owners to check for blue-green algae, which blooms in late summer in certain ponds throughout the area and on Cape Cod. The toxic algae can kill a dog that drinks just a small amount of the poisoned pond water.

When owners take a few precautions to ensure their pet's health during the warmer weather, everyone will have a safe, healthy and enjoyable summer.

NEW BOOK IS INDEED THE CAT'S MEOW

Do you want to be a better cat owner?

Oftentimes feline fanciers have questions of a non-veterinary nature regarding behavior, grooming, training and other issues, and need factual, well-researched information that is difficult to find.

In her new book, *The Complete Cat's Meow* (Wiley, 2011), pet writer and television personality Darlene Arden equips pet owners, shelter volunteers and foster caregivers with sound advice and important information necessary to give kittens a wonderful head start to become great pets and beloved members of the family.

The 256-page comprehensive book also contains plenty of wisdom about caring for mature cats and senior felines. Arden conducted research for the book by interviewing responsible purebred cat breeders to discover how they successfully raise happy and healthy felines that are a joy to own.

"Even experienced owners will learn some new things," Arden begins. "My goal by writing this book is to make cats' lives better and to improve the human-animal bond. It's an all-in-one cat guide."

Arden, a certified animal behavior consultant, offers countless tips that will make caring for Fluffy easier and less stressful. When trimming nails, for example, Arden says many cats become agitated because they think that the groomer, who is dominant in this situation, is taking away something.

"Do what makes the cat happy," Arden advises, suggesting that although some cats can get all of their nails trimmed in one session, other felines can only tolerate having one nail trimmed per day.

The author adds that owners should always praise their cat verbally when the animal is being groomed.

"Always give the cat a treat after nail trimming," Arden continues, adding that the feline will learn to associate the procedure with a positive reward.

The book offers an online link to a video that offers a step-by-step demonstration of nail trimming, one of the many videos that Arden suggests owners watch to learn more about feline care.

The respected writer reveals that litter box issues can easily resolved if owners will invest the time and patience to work with the cat.

"The rule of thumb is one for the house, and one for each cat," she says.

Arden recommends that since cats like their privacy, owners in multi-cat households should never place litter boxes in a row.

"Keep them in different places around the house and place one litter box on each floor," she adds.

The author also dispels many popular myths about felines that folks have believed for centuries.

"A black cat crossing the street is just going somewhere," Arden laughs.

"Contrary to what many people believe, cats can be trained," Arden emphasizes, recommending that kitten owners should start teaching their new pet as soon as the animal is introduced to its new home.

"Cats learn a lot faster than dogs," she notes, adding that felines can be taught to come when called, lie down, shake hands and perform many other cute tricks. Arden also reveals that owners should ignore bad behavior and reward good manners.

"Your kitty will soon understand what gets him the attention he seeks," she explains.

Although Arden offers chapters on health and nutrition, she emphasizes that the book is not a substitute for veterinary care. She urges owners to work in cooperation with small-animal practitioners to develop a comprehensive wellness plan that best suits the animal's individual needs.

"Talk to your vet about proper diet," the author advises, noting that all cats, especially obese felines, need exercise. Indoor cats can keep in shape by tossing catnip mice or chasing a feather toy, and outdoor cats that need to lose weight can be placed in a harness and walked around the yard several times a day when the weather is mild and not humid.

Another way to exercise a portly feline is to toss a few pieces of kibble a short distance up the stairs and let the cat run after the edible reward.

The pet expert says it's important for cat owners to regularly check for fleas and other parasites, and open wounds that need medical treatment. Arden urges prospective cat owners not to purchase or adopt a longhaired cat without making a commitment to regular brushing.

"Start gently and keep it up daily," she advises, adding that cats are meticulous and take pride in their appearance.

Although much of Arden's advice is geared toward owners of kittens and young cats, she strongly advocates for the adoption of adult felines.

"I encourage many people to adopt an older cat," she says, adding that mature cats make "wonderful friends."

Arden emphasizes that many folks, because of work schedules and other responsibilities, often don't have the time it takes to properly train a curious kitten.

"When you adopt an older cat, what you see is what you get," the author concludes.

IT'S TIME FOR THE TUXEDO CROWD

Imagine two dozen feisty Boston Terriers swiftly running and leaping like graceful gazelles darting across a grassy field while their owners laugh and exchange the latest news about their dogs and their beloved breed.

Although the scene might look like a clip from *Animal Planet* or a photograph from the pages of *National Geographic*, it's actually just another Sunday morning gathering of the Westport (Massachusetts) Boston Terrier Meetup Group, a local gathering of breed fanciers who like to have fun with their dogs.

On the second Sunday of most months, the Boston Terrier enthusiasts gather at Massachusetts' Freetown State Forest at 10 a.m. for a couple of hours of play, followed by a hike on the preserve's wooded trails. In warmer weather, the group meets at a local beach where the dogs cool off and frolic in the shallow water.

The group was the brainchild of Linda Bramwell, a Westport resident, who was looking for another Boston Terrier to socialize with her dog Rocky.

"It took a while to get started," Bramwell recalls, noting that she placed a short advertisement in 2007 on www.meetup.com, an Internet website that helps people with similar interests connect and plan activities. The group now has dozens of members from all over the South Coast of Massachusetts as well as Rhode Island.

"The dogs look forward to it," Bramwell continues. "We're all Boston Terrier lovers."

Bramwell now owns three of the playful canines, known for their distinctive black and white "tuxedo" markings, alert expression and erect ears.

According to the American Kennel Club, the Boston Terrier is truly an "All-American" dog. The lively, loyal breed was developed after the Civil War in the stables of Boston as a fighting dog, and resulted from a cross between an English Bulldog and a white English Terrier.

The Boston Terrier is the official state dog of Massachusetts and now serves primarily as a family companion. The breed ranked 23rd in popularity last year, according to AKC registration records, and should weigh no more than 25 pounds, although most specimens tip the scales at less than 20 pounds.

One of the Boston's most distinguishing characteristics, aside from its unique square head and jaw, is the breed's friendly disposition. Except for a few minor skirmishes, the dogs that attended a recent Freetown event played well together and seemed to enjoy each other's company. In fact, the playgroup was like a big family reunion.

For Judy Mathieu of Somerset, Massachusetts, the monthly gatherings offer a special opportunity to see many of the enthusiastic young Bostons her dog Lilly gave birth to more than a year ago. Eight of the nine puppies survived in a litter considered "huge" for such a small breed. Many of the littermates were sold to area families who regularly attend the sessions and share colorful stories of their dogs' antics and advice about caring for these handsome canines.

"It was amazing," says Mathieu of the large brood. "She was the best mother in the world."

When David Laberge of Dartmouth, Massachusetts purchased one of the tiny puppies, little did he know that the dog he named Max would soon become his pride and joy.

"I was always interested in the Boston Terrier," Laberge admits, describing his canine companion as a "high energy and active dog" that complements his owner's busy lifestyle.

"It's an excellent mix," he continues, adding that Max likes to play in the surf and retrieves a favorite toy ball.

"He's a nature boy," Laberge reveals, adding that the only drawback to owning a Boston Terrier is that the dogs snore loudly when they sleep.

One of the playgroup's most ardent supporters is Robyn Peters, an Acushnet, Massachusetts resident who owns four delightful Boston Terriers.

"They grab my attention," the dog lover reveals. "Boston Terriers are a special breed and they have huge personalities. They think they're human."

Peters notes that she's made many friends in the special group, which has no dues or special requirements other than a love for Boston Terriers. She adds that owners readily share tips on feeding, training, and medical issues such as skin conditions that can often irritate these otherwise healthy canines.

"This is just a big Boston Terrier family," Peters concludes. "We look forward to seeing each other every month."

For more information about the Westport Boston Terrier Meetup Group, visit www.meetup.com/boston-terrier-social/.

KEEP FIDO OUT OF THE POUND

Animal shelter officials throughout the United States continue to report that these facilities are overflowing with beautiful dogs waiting to be adopted. Many are purebred, most are healthy, and all just need a second chance.

Although many experts blame the economy for the influx, others attribute the surge to dogs being relinquished because of improper training, inadequate care and unrealistic expectations. Sadly, some inexperienced owners believe that dogs will train themselves or won't grow any larger than the tiny ball of fluff that once fit on a child's lap.

Pet writer Lexianne Grant says one common mistake made by many first-time dog owners is that they expect the new family pet to be just like their friend's well-trained canine companion or like a great dog that steals their hearts in a movie. Every dog is not Lassie or Rin Tin Tin!

"They don't realize that it takes time to develop that behavior and bond; then when they have a puppy, they are totally bewildered why their dog isn't perfect," she begins. "These buyers sometimes see pets as disposable entertainment and get rid of the pet when the going gets rough, when the animal needs time or attention."

Grant, a Norwegian Elkhound fancier, says she's witnessed this unfortunate situation many times through her volunteer work in breed adoption programs.

"I've seen this in rescue, usually with puppies age 7-months and older, or in a slightly older dog that's gone berserk because it's been neglected most if its life," she notes.

Grant says that many new owners who surrender a dog to a shelter after a few months often make the mistake of failing to appreciate the human-animal bond, or are simply unaware of how to care for a dependent creature.

"The solution is to read about dog care and behavior prior to making the purchase," she advises, adding that if problems continue to develop after the dog settles into its new home, there are many options that can be implemented to correct bad behavior, such as obedience training.

Once an owner commits to caring for an animal, a positive relationship develops, Grant emphasizes.

The respected author says another common misconception is that many new dog owners think once a canine is trained, the animal will never have an accident in the house again.

"Welcome to the world of dogs where poop and piddle fill your days," Grant says, chuckling, adding that even the most reliable dog can have an accident indoors if the poor creature becomes sick or frightened.

Grant says one way for potential owners to obtain a more realistic view of responsible pet ownership is to visit friends and family members and observe how they feed and clean up after their dog, as well as how they care for the animal when it's recuperating from surgery or an illness.

Fall River, Massachusetts resident and longtime animal advocate Joyce Pinsonnault recalls that when she adopted Nina, a Chihuahua-Pug-mix from that city's Forever Paws Animal Shelter several months ago, the dog "lacked proper training" and still can be a handful.

"She was 13-months-old and still hadn't been house trained," Pinsonnault, a shelter board member, remembers. "I wanted a dog that I could live with and could live with others."

The experienced dog owner and former veterinary technician says although it took four months to housebreak the tiny dog, Nina still has a few behavioral issues.

"We are still working on them," Pinsonnault admits. "She was always very loving and that's why I took her."

Darlene Arden, author of *The Angell Memorial Animal Hospital Book of Wellness and Preventative Care for Dogs*, says one common mistake made by many novice dog owners is that they are not fully prepared to make a lifetime commitment to the animal. She adds that although every puppy is cute, owners should also realize that the animal is genetically programmed to perform a task, such as working, herding or hunting.

"Puppies need to have their energy properly channeled and adult dogs need exercise, and usually a job," Arden emphasizes. "Positive training and getting involved in a dog sport is the perfect answer to both. You will strengthen the human-animal bond and have a better behaved dog by putting some time and energy into the relationship right at the beginning."

Arden says once the dog matures, it's important to stay involved in an activity such as obedience, flyball, agility, rally or earthdog trials for terriers and Dachshunds. Those pursuits provide recreation and exercise both for owners and their canine pals, and also keep a dog mentally stimulated.

"The bonus is that you'll meet other like-minded people," she says.

WITH PROPER CARE, DIABETIC CATS CAN LEAD NORMAL LIVES

There's good news for cats suffering from diabetes. Veterinary experts are reassuring owners of affected felines that with proper diet, medication and careful supervision, these animals can lead long and relatively normal lives.

"The best way to avoid diabetes is to keep the cat's weight normal," begins Dr. Tim Donovan, owner of Kindred Spirits Mobile Veterinary Services in Mattapoisett, Massachusetts. "Any cat can develop diabetes, but obese cats are more at risk."

Like humans, most cats that develop the disorder suffer from Type 2 or adult onset diabetes, which is sometimes known as a lifestyle disease because those affected are overweight and often sedentary.

Donovan believes that a low-carbohydrate diet provides protection against the treatable disease.

"That means dry food should be avoided, and cats should eat a paté-style canned food," he advises. "This food most closely replicates the cats' natural carnivorous diet."

The respected veterinarian reports that although there is no gender predisposition to diabetes, he treats more males than females, and adds that there is a high incidence of the disease in "orange ale" (orange-colored) tabbies. That phenomenon has led Donovan to believe that some felines might have a genetic predisposition to developing the medical condition.

Although younger cats can develop diabetes, the disease usually affects more middle-aged cats because it takes the creatures longer to become obese.

Father Fred Babiczuk, pastor of Good Shepherd Parish in Fall River, Massachusetts notes that his cat Gateway was diagnosed with diabetes more than three years ago.

"He looks like a Gateway computer box," the cat-loving priest acknowledges, describing the large black and white cartons designed to resemble a Holstein cow.

Father Babiczuk describes the middle-aged cat as a "big boy." The hefty feline tips the scale at 19 pounds, and is much larger than the priest's other cats, Minnie and Orphan Annie. All three felines were adopted after they were found wandering near Father Babiczuk's family home in Taunton.

The priest recalls that he became concerned when Gateway began losing weight and drinking lots of water, which resulted in frequent trips to the litter box.

Medical tests confirmed Father Babiczuk's suspicions, and the feline was immediately placed on human-grade insulin to control the diabetes.

"His sugar was very high," the cat owner remembers, adding that he was taught by Gateway's veterinarian how to inject the medication without causing discomfort. The diabetic cat receives 8 units of insulin in the morning and 7 units at night into the scruff of the neck.

Father Babiczuk says it's a lot easier taking care of a diabetic cat than it is caring for a human with a similar condition.

"He gets treats after the injections," the pastor reveals. "If I forget to give him his shot, he comes running."

According to Father Babiczuk, the handsome feline eats a regular diet, and like most cats, enjoys a small serving of baked fish as a special treat. Gateway's favorites are tuna and salmon.

"He's more prone to infections," the cat owner continues, noting that owners of diabetic cats and dogs have to be observant and pay close attention to their animals. When infections develop, immediate veterinary intervention is required to prevent the illness from spreading or causing possible organ damage.

Father Babiczuk has Gateway's blood glucose level tested every two months.

"His numbers have been very good," he says. Normal blood glucose values for non-diabetic cats and dogs range from 80 to 150 as measured on a vet's glucometer. When Gateway was first tested three years ago, the feline's blood glucose level was almost 400, which could have caused serious complications if left untreated.

"Having a diabetic cat is not that difficult," Father Babiczuk emphasizes, adding that he spends about $220 annually for needles and insulin, which he obtains from a retail pharmacy with a prescription from Gateway's veterinarian.

The priest estimates he spends an additional $100 a year for bi-monthly glucose tests.

"He's very easy going," Father Babiczuk says of his feline friend. "If someone comes into the rectory, he just sits there. He's the king; he's not going to be put out by anyone."

MALAMUTES KNOWN FOR LOYALTY AND STRENGTH

One of the few indigenous American breeds is the Alaskan Malamute, a powerful Arctic dog known for its unfailing loyalty and strength.

The oldest member of the sled dog group, this large working breed is a cousin of the Samoyed, Siberian Husky and American Eskimo dog.

According to breed historians, the Alaskan Malamute was named for a native Inuit tribe called the Mahlemuts, who inhabited the shores of Kotzebue Sound in the upper-western part of Alaska many centuries ago. The natives employed these dogs to haul sledges, large sleds that were used to transport freight between villages over icy and snowy terrain.

Last year, the Mal ranked 57th in popularity, according to American Kennel Club registration statistics, a slight decline from 2002 when it was the nation's 53rd most popular breed.

Acushnet resident and sled dog fancier Donna Lopes is having a lot of fun with her second Malamute, a six-year-old male affectionately known as Brody, although the dog's official registered name is Kloudburst Nantucket Knight.

Lopes, who owned and trained Siberian Huskies for many years, says she wanted a different Arctic breed several years ago and fell in love with the Malamute when she encountered a male being exhibited at a dog show.

"He was just so beautiful, and he had a good temperament," the dog lover recalls, adding that she quickly put her name on a waiting list for a puppy.

"They are a big dog," she continues, noting that these rugged, alert dogs were "bred to go long distances pulling heavy weights" often in harsh weather conditions when travel can be perilous.

"They have a lot of endurance and strength and they love to work," Lopes says, adding that despite being dedicated to their job, most Malamutes are very friendly and make good family companions.

According to canine historians and breed experts, the Malamute is heavier boned than the Husky. The larger dog was bred to pull large loads over short distances, and its smaller cousin was developed to pull lighter loads on longer treks. Unlike Huskies, which have a variety of eye colors, including blue, all Mals have dark brown eyes.

Lopes reports that Brody has earned Canine Good Citizen, Beginner Novice obedience and Rally Novice and Rally Advanced titles, and will continue training in the fall to pursue a Companion Dog degree and a Rally Excellence title. Lopes trains the dog in obedience with Jeanie Crosby at Jeanie's Education Center in Marion, Massachusetts and attends rally classes offered by Robin Botelho at the Wampanoag Kennel Club in nearby Acushnet.

"He loves rally," Lopes says, noting that the challenging set of obedience and heeling exercises and jumps require Brody to always contemplate his next move. "These dogs love to work."

She emphasizes that like all dogs, Malamutes must be trained as puppies and can become easily bored without some sort of activity as they mature.

"They need to have their mind stimulated," Lopes says. "I have never seen a smarter dog."

The sled dog fancier adds that Mals sometimes try to get away with things and have their own way.

"They can be head strong and stubborn, but if you establish yourself as the leader and are consistent and patient they can be excellent family pets and very loyal companions," Lopes notes.

According to Lopes, it's easier than most people think to keep the Arctic breed comfortable during the summer. The dog owner keeps the air conditioner on all day during warm weather, and lets Brody enjoy a refreshing daily romp in a large children's pool.

"He loves to swim," she says, adding that the athletic dog also likes to take a walk on the beach and enjoys splashing in the waves. These dogs require a great deal of exercise and are not a good companion for a sedentary owner.

Lopes reveals that the big dog sheds profusely in late spring, when it loses its thick cotton-like undercoat, and again in the fall, when the dog's thinner summer coat falls out. These canines only require two baths a year, since frequent bathing will result in the loss of essential natural oils that prevent the coat from becoming dry and brittle.

"They stay very clean," Lopes says, adding that the dogs are like cats and groom their own coats, although most owners give their dogs a periodic brushing.

Although the Alaskan Malamute is generally very healthy, the breed is prone to developing bloat, and can be affected by hip dysplasia. Dogs that are not properly socialized as puppies can be aggressive toward other dogs.

Lopes says that Mals don't bark or howl, like most other canines.

"They 'woo-woo' as a form of a communication," she says, adding that some dogs are very vocal, like Timber, the first Malamute Lopes owned.

"Mals are not for everyone," Lopes advises, urging prospective owners "to research the breed to see if it is a good fit for their lifestyle and to find a reputable breeder."

If the Mal is a good match, the sled dog fan says, you'll gain a loyal family companion whose affection and unconditional love will provide great rewards.

SOME GOOD NEWS FOR CAT OWNERS

The good news for cat owners is that our feline friends are living longer and healthier lives.

Veterinary experts report that with preventative medicine, regular veterinary checkups and good nutrition, a domesticated cat can live to age 18 or longer.

Daisy, my tiger cat, celebrated her 18th birthday on April 1, 2010 and enjoyed a hearty meal and chasing field mice. At the time of her birthday, the sleek feline was in good health and often acted like a precocious kitten.

"It's becoming more and more common for cats to live into their late teens," says Amy Shojai, author of *Complete Care for Your Aging Cat* and past president of the Cat Writers of America.

"It's not unusual for cats to lives into their 20s," she continues. "Cats that have received good preventative care for a decade or more benefit at the back end of their lives as much as during their youth."

Shojai reveals that although some cat breeds tend to be longer-lived than others, "the average for old these days has stretched upwards." Well-cared for cats are enjoying longer lives than their ancestors.

"Pet food companies used to say cats were senior at age 7 and geriatric at ages 12 to 14," the feline expert discloses. "These days I wouldn't consider a cat to be senior until age 10, and geriatric at 14 years old or above."

She says it's important for owners to be proactive to help ensure that a cat survives to enjoy its golden years.

"Simply keeping the kitty at a healthy weight — or even a bit thin — increases longevity," Shojai reveals. "Less is better."

The popular radio and television talk show guest reports that more than 70 percent of all cats by age 4 have developed periodontal disease, which can affect heart, kidney and liver function and the animal's general health.

"Keeping teeth clean can be very positive," she advises.

Shojai, an award-winning author of more than 23 pet books, says new research indicates that up to 90 percent of cats age 10 and older suffer from painful arthritis. Overweight cats often suffer debilitating joint pain and are at greater risk of developing feline diabetes, which can be fatal if not properly treated with medication prescribed by a veterinarian.

"Keeping cats active with play helps lubricate the joints to reduce pain, and also keeps weight off," she continues. "Interactive play helps, and also think about using food puzzles to encourage cats to 'mimic' hunting behavior and get off their furry tails."

Since cats are prone to developing cognitive disorders or "kitty Alzheimer's" as they age, Shojai tells owners to make their cat "think" instead of allowing the animal to become a lazy couch potato.

"Exercising the mind with games and puzzle toys, clicker training and more can delay or in some cases, prevent the onset of this disorder," she notes.

Although some owners contend that indoor cats live longer than felines allowed outdoors, veterinary experts often disagree. They argue that many indoor cats, although protected from traffic and preying animals, may have their lives shortened by obesity, lack of exercise and stress created by boredom.

Shojai states that improvements in veterinary medicine parallel advances made in human treatment.

"Pretty much anything available in human medicine also can be done for cats," Shojai says. "Diagnostic tests today include MRI, CT-scans, ultrasound, gene-therapy and testing, brain surgeries, radioactive iodine (for hyperthyroid), cataract repair, kidney transplants, advanced cancer options and more."

Other developments include improvements in vaccinations that prevent diseases, new parasite medications, nutritional advances that maintain health or reverse the progression of certain medical conditions and behavioral medications to help keep pets calm.

Pet writer and cat fancier Catherine Fitch says caring for an elderly cat requires patience and a lot of money if the animal becomes sick and needs long-term veterinary care.

The author's cat, KoKo, a 15-year-old flame point Siamese, suffers from megacolon, a severe form of constipation that occurs when the colon loses its flexibility. Stools become large and are difficult to pass.

"We have him on a special diet that includes chicken and chicken livers mixed with a special supplement," Fitch says, adding that the feline also takes laxatives twice daily.

"He has also had to go to the veterinarian for enemas on numerous occasions," the writer notes, describing the visits as "expensive outings" because KoKo doesn't cooperate and has to be anesthetized.

Although KoKo's medical condition is managed fairly well, the feline still gets impacted about once every other month and requires additional laxatives until the stool is passed.

"He gets miserable and cranky and vomits, so of course we recognize symptoms right away," Fitch adds, revealing that the painful condition is not uncommon in cats.

"I've wanted to have him put to sleep on occasion," she admits. "I just get so tired of dealing with it. It is expensive, and I also feel terribly sorry for him. My husband cannot stand to have him put down."

YOUNG STUDENT DEDICATED TO ANIMALS

Faith Trezon isn't your typical fourth grader.

Like many children, the 10-year-old New Bedford, Massachusetts resident loves animals and takes great care of her family's pets. What makes the talented student unique is her dedication to homeless animals that aren't as lucky as her two beloved cats and affectionate little dog named Bella.

For the past two years, the young animal advocate and humanitarian has conducted fundraisers to benefit C.A.R.E. South Coast (Center for Animal Rescue and Education), a local volunteer organization that provides shelter to homeless animals, spay and neuter assistance, public education and vital referral resources.

Faith learned about the shelter while attending Pet Photos with Santa in 2011 at Capeway Veterinary Hospital in Fairhaven, where she met shelter representatives who were sponsoring the holiday event. After visiting the facility, and witnessing firsthand the plight of several homeless animals, Faith embarked on a mission to raise funds and collect supplies to benefit the shelter, which relies on community support to care for its burgeoning population of less-fortunate creatures.

"I love pets very much," Faith begins. "I've wanted to become a veterinarian since I was four years old."

Last year, Faith asked her mother Corie Trezon to write a letter to Pulaski Elementary School Principal Tammy Morgan seeking permission to hold a fundraiser to benefit the facility, which is located at 596 Hathaway Road, New Bedford.

Morgan allowed the enterprising student to make announcements over the intercom, and Faith, realizing that the 100th day of the school year was fast approaching, created the slogan, "100 Days,

100 Ways to make a Difference for Homeless Animals" which she displayed on posters to announce the appeal.

Faith's altruism and the outstanding support she received from the Pulaski community resulted in a $287 cash donation and about $500 worth of supplies to help improve the lives of homeless cats and dogs entrusted to the shelter's care.

Building on her previous success, Faith, seeking to develop a "tradition," sought permission a few weeks ago to conduct a similar campaign. With Morgan's enthusiastic support, all the Pulaski students participated in a classroom challenge with the goal of having each class donate 100 items to commemorate the 100th day of school.

Despite missing a few days of the two-week campaign because of illness, and three additional days as a result of a blizzard, Faith remained diligent and raised $312 and approximately $800 in food and other supplies. Contributors also included family members, friends and supportive neighbors.

As part of the fundraiser, Faith also created a "Paw Pouch," a mini-purse fashioned out of duct-tape that she sold for $5.

"People have been very generous, and it makes a difference," the passionate student observes, adding that she hopes her efforts will inspire other students to embrace a cause and make a positive contribution to the community.

Faith says the project has motivated her to plan a veterinary career working in a shelter where she can make a significant difference in the lives of animals cast aside by society.

Principal Morgan says the young animal fancier "shows a lot of motivation. She's done all of the legwork. She wanted to make a difference."

Noting that the school's theme for April is "self-discipline," Morgan says Faith's community involvement shows "a lot of initiative and a lot of drive."

The educator added that the compassionate student was recently presented with the Pulaski Pride Award at a school-wide assembly to acknowledge her ingenuity.

"This is only the beginning of things to come," the educator predicts, adding that she hopes other students will follow Faith's example and become leaders in their communities. The fundraiser has also garnered the support of Faith's younger brother, Devin, a third grader, who proudly told his classmates about his sister's worthy project.

Corie Trezon describes her daughter as a "true humanitarian. I feel very proud and grateful that my daughter wants to make a difference. She's a very caring and genuine girl."

Noting that her daughter took the initiative to start the project and did most of the work, Trezon adds that all she did was write the letters to the school principal, purchase the poster board and, together with her husband Steve, deliver the monetary donations and supplies to the shelter.

Ruth Marshman, president of C.A.R.E. South Coast, marvels at Faith's commitment to homeless animals. "It's inspiring how someone so young cares so much about what we do," Marshman says. "Her dedication is amazing."

The shelter leader hopes that Faith's efforts will inspire other like-minded youngsters who are too young to volunteer at the facility because of insurance liability, to nonetheless support C.A.R.E. South Coast's programs by holding fundraisers to help make a positive difference in the lives of homeless pets.

FROSTBITE: DON'T LEAVE PETS OUTDOORS IN FREEZING WEATHER

Veterinary experts are warning owners to take precautions to prevent pets from developing frostbite as the thermostat continues to plummet and Mother Nature blankets the region with ice and snow.

"Frostbite is a result of an animal staying in the frigid outside for a longer period of time than it should," explains Dr. Philip Gaudet, owner of Capeway Veterinary Hospital of Fairhaven, Massachusetts. He adds that a cat or dog's extremities, including the ears, toes, tail and genitals are in danger of freezing when the animal is exposed to freezing temperatures for more than a few minutes.

"This is the worst and most rapid way to interrupt the blood supply to those body parts," the respected veterinarian continues. "In the recent weather we have experienced, these dangers have been, and will continue to be, real and urgent matters for pets and their owners."

Gaudet notes that frostbite can occur at and just below the freezing point or 32° Fahrenheit. He adds that although shorthaired or smooth-coated animals, such as Pugs and Whippets, are more prone to freezing than longhaired pets, all creatures can be affected.

"Of course, Husky-like pets will fare better than Chihuahuas and their short-coated relations," the small-animal practitioner emphasizes.

Noting that the time it takes for frostbite to develop depends on the ambient temperature, he warns that if it's below freezing, a few minutes can make a difference.

"Let them urinate and defecate and get them inside!" Gaudet advises. "Better yet, if possible, set up a small, easily cleaned, papered area in the house for your pet to soil."

The veterinarian reports that when frostbite initially occurs, a cat or dog's extremities are frozen. As the body parts defrost, the extremities will first become warm and painful, then swollen and very tender when touched. If not properly treated, the tissue gradually becomes stiff and hard, with a texture similar to old leather or cardboard, and eventually begins to flake and peel away from the skin like a scab.

"Underneath may be more dead tissue, or an open wound," Gaudet warns. "Ear tips and tails will rot off and may expose the cartilage or tailbone. Toes and sometimes lower legs are similarly affected. The prepuce (penis sheath) can also freeze."

Gaudet says that treatment of frostbite is initially a matter of returning the tissues to a normal body temperature, which lies in the range of 100.5° to 102.5° F for both cats and dogs.

"A soft massage with your bare hands or cool, moist cloths will slowly return any tissue to body temperature," he advises. "Sometimes a simple antibiotic and good nursing care is all that is necessary. In some cases, surgical intervention (amputation) is required."

Noted author and columnist Amy Shojai reveals that cats are actually "a bit more savvy than dogs when it comes to cold weather" and generally seek shelter more quickly.

"Cats tuck their feet under the belly so toes may not be affected as often," Shojai says, but she warns that ear tips and tails are at risk because those extremities are exposed even when a feline is curled into a ball.

Shojai, the author of more than 23 pet care books, including *The First-Aid Companion for Dogs and Cats*, says frostbite can be difficult to detect when the typical pale white, gray or blue color of frozen skin is hidden by fur. She adds that even the Nordic breeds, such as uskies and Finnish Spitz, can suffer from frostbite.

"Pets may limp from frozen toes, frozen ear tops tend to droop and the skin will be very cold, hard and non-pliable," she says.

Shojai says it's imperative that outdoor pets have proper shelter from the wind and cold, or the animal could die. She emphasizes that the size of the shelter should only be slightly larger than the pet's body so the animal can be warmed by its own body heat.

"Even better, keep your cats and dogs inside and avoid the risk altogether," she concludes.

DELIGHTFUL, INTELLIGENT COCKER SPANIELS BRING MUCH JOY

Do you know what breed is known as "the smallest member of the sporting dog family?"

If you said, "The Cocker Spaniel," you're right!

This popular breed is a descendent of early land spaniels, which were developed in England during the 14th century. Cockers were the smallest of these indigenous dogs, and earned their name from the breed's proficiency to flush woodcock from the thrushes and retrieve fallen birds on command.

The breed has been exhibited in this country since the early 1880s. These early dogs resembled the larger English Cocker Spaniel that we also see today. During the early 20th century, American fanciers wanted a more agile spaniel and developed a smaller variety that differed in type, size and color.

Sportsmen quickly took to these versatile, enthusiastic hunting dogs, and field trials were established for the breed during the 1920s. Hunters continue to prize these dogs for their ability to cover all types of terrain within gun range with speed and dexterity, flushing game birds and retrieving on command in water as well as on land.

Some dog show exhibitors, working diligently to also preserve the Cocker's inherent hunting ability, also train their dogs in the field, often after the animal has retired from the conformation ring. Hundreds of Cockers have earned AKC junior and master hunting titles.

Other fanciers, drawn by the Cocker Spaniel's handsome appearance and delightful temperament, purchase these lively sporting dogs as family pets. The Cocker's popularity has steadily grown during the past half century, and last year, the Cocker Spaniel ranked in the top 20 in the number of dogs registered with the AKC.

Swansea, Massachusetts resident Gail Zurawski has owned Cocker Spaniels for 18 years.

"I always wanted one," the experienced dog owner reveals. "I wanted a buff puppy, but I couldn't find one, so I bought a black and white parti-colored Cocker and I fell in love with them."

Zurawski has owned three parti-colored Cockers and plans to buy another puppy in the fall. She purchases her dogs from respected kennels, and trains the canines in obedience in classes conducted by the Wampanoag Kennel Club.

"All three of my Cockers have earned obedience degrees," she notes.

The knowledgeable trainer says that two of her canines, Heidi and Gretchen, both deceased, earned Companion Dog titles, and her current charge, Lily, has earned a Canine Good Citizen title, Therapy Dog certification and a Companion Dog Excellent degree, the equivalent of a master's degree.

Although Lilly no longer competes because of diminished eyesight, the energetic canine hasn't lost her joie de vivre.

"She is a people person," Zurawski relates. "She loves kids."

The dog owner says that the friendly spaniel also likes to visit nursing homes.

"Lilly climbs up in bed with some of the residents, and she once jumped right up on the lap of a man who was sitting in a wheelchair."

Zurawski says that obedience training has been has been beneficial to the elderly and almost blind dog. Most Cocker Spaniels enjoy a lifespan of 12 to 14 years.

"It has helped her with many things," the owner notes, adding that the small spaniel can jump into the car and maneuver stairs with little difficulty.

"She comes when she hears my voice," Zurawski adds.

Structurally, the Cocker Spaniel has a sturdy, compact body and a cleanly chiseled and refined head. Specimens should be well-balanced and possess a typical, effortless sporting dog gait. Cockers should always be alert and cover ground with ease.

Zurawski emphasizes that Cocker Spaniels are usually fastidious indoors and don't shed excessively but do require regular brushing and grooming. Outdoors, Cockers like to chase birds and other animals, so owners should have a fenced-in yard.

According to the approved breed standard, a Cocker Spaniel may be black or black with tan points, ASCOB (any solid color other than black), which ranges from light cream to deep red, chocolate or chocolate with tan points, or parti-colored — two or more solid, well-broken colors — one of which must be white.

Although some poorly bred Cocker Spaniels of all three varieties can have poor temperaments, the breed standard states that dispositions should be "even" and these dogs should never be timid or aggressive.

"I think that the parti-colored dogs have better temperaments than the ASCOB or black dogs," Zurawski believes, adding that she's heard reports that some owners have had problems socializing buff-colored dogs.

"Each Cocker has brought me a lot of joy," the longtime spaniel owner concludes. "I can't wait to get my next puppy and start training."

PERUVIAN BREED CERTAINLY DRAWS ATTENTION

If you want a dog that's going to turn heads, the Peruvian Inca Orchid just might be the perfect choice.

These unusual hairless or short-coated sighthounds are very rare in this country and always attract a lot of attention.

Westport, Massachusetts resident and P.I.O. owner Darlene Dimor says that even at dog shows, experienced fanciers and professional handlers stop and ask about Kat, her six-month-old hairless canine who resembles a punk rocker.

Kat has pink skin with mahogany-colored spots and sports short tuffs of hair on her head and tail.

Dimor, a longtime Pharaoh Hound breeder and successful exhibitor, began searching for a hairless breed about 10 years ago. She and her husband Phil wanted a smaller breed to complement the large sighthounds that they have owned for many years.

"The P.I.O. has the moxie to co-exist with the Pharaohs," Dimor begins, adding that when Kat matures, the sleek canine will be the size of a Whippet and will weigh about 26 pounds.

According to the breed standard, the Peruvian Inca Orchid has three varieties: small, 9¾ to 15¾ inches at the withers; medium, 15¾ to 19¾ inches; and large, 19¾ to 25¾ inches. Weight is in relation to the size, with males weighing proportionately more than females, and can range from 8½ to 55 pounds, depending on the size and gender of the animal.

Breed historians report that the hairless variety was valued by pre-Incan cultures and later by the Incas, who locked coated dogs indoors at sundown, and allowed the hairless canines to run outside to get exercise. The two types were kept apart, which resulted in a small hairless gene pool that is most likely responsible for the incomplete dentition in the smooth dogs, a trait that scientists have linked to the hairless gene.

When the Spanish conquered the coastal areas of Peru almost 500 years ago, they discovered hairless hounds living in the houses of the Incas among colorful night-blooming orchid blossoms and romantically named the dogs Perros Flora, which translates to "flower dog." The name later changed to Moonflower Dog, and today the graceful, willowy hound is called the Peruvian Inca Orchid in the United States and parts of Europe where they are kept in small numbers.

Canine geneticists believe that there may have been early crosses of native species and small greyhounds brought from Europe by the Conquistadors, which reinforced the sighthound characteristics of the Peruvian hairless dogs.

Dimor adds that in Peru, the unique dogs were used as bed warmers or to relieve arthritic pain.

"They feel just like a hot water bottle," she says, adding that in ancient times, the dogs were prized by wealthy families. "They are warm to the touch."

Veterinary experts reveal that although the P.I.O. has the same body temperature as any other breed, the lack of hair makes the dog feel warmer.

Since the hairless dogs have no insulation, Dimor dresses Kat in a light doggie sweater to keep warm when the dog is indoors, and a heavier canine coat when the elegant hound goes outside in cold weather to exercise. Breeders recommend applying sunscreen during summer to avoid sunburn.

The respected dog fancier discloses that Kat, whose registered name is Xcel's Blue Moon Katchina, doesn't enjoy being left alone.

"These dogs like to be with their family," Dimor continues. "They like the attention."

Although these fragile canines are primarily kept as household pets, the athletic P.I.O. loves to chase game and excels at lure coursing.

"You don't have to train these dogs," Dimor says, adding that the agile canine is a natural runner.

Of the five females born in Kat's litter, only two were hairless. Although the breed standard emphasizes that the hairless variety must have prick or erect ears, coated dogs are permitted to have floppy ears. Dimor says that although most prick ears develop naturally, sometimes breeders tape them — like Dobermans or Boxers — as puppies mature.

Experts report that the hairless variety does not attract fleas and requires a weekly bath, but the coated dogs, whose furnishings can range from short to medium in length, require regular brushing to keep the coat free of debris and parasites.

"They are absolutely a fun dog," Dimor adds. "Kat is a little clown. They love to play."

The proud dog owner reveals that the unique hound had no trouble getting used to its much larger Pharaoh Hound cousins.

"She's the boss," Dimor observes. "She uses the Pharaoh Hounds like a mattress or a pillow. They are nice and toasty."

Although the Peruvian Inca Orchid has enjoyed a long and colorful history, perhaps the latest chapter is the most interesting. Several years ago, when the Peruvian government realized the breed, which is Peru's only internationally registered dog, was in danger of extinction, officials elected to preserve the breed by mandating all archeological sites along the coast to have at least one pair on location.

"They're not there as guard dogs but as part of the historical scenery," reports author and breed historian Alice Bixler in a recent e-mail. "They greet tourists entering the museums during the day and when the sites close down for the evening, they scamper along the walls of the ruins, just as they did so many centuries ago."

DOES FLUFFY NEED A DIET?

Do you own a tubby tabby or a pooch that has packed on a few pounds?

According to veterinary experts, pet obesity has become a major concern in treating cats and dogs, and may be a contributing cause of many serious and debilitating health issues.

Dr. Ted Sherman, co-owner of Capeway Veterinary Hospital in Fairhaven, Massachusetts, reports that when he began practicing 30 years ago, he'd guess that only five to seven percent of his four-footed patients were overweight.

"Currently I would estimate 85 percent of my patients to be obese," he reports. Sherman defines obesity as a medical condition in which excess body fat has accumulated to the extent that it may have an adverse effect on health, leading to reduced life expectancy and/or increased medical problems.

The veterinarian, a graduate of Louisiana State University, thinks obesity is slightly more prevalent in dogs than cats, as felines will play by themselves up to an older age than dogs will, and they tend to free roam more often than their canine counterparts. Like humans, all cats and dogs need regular exercise and stimulation to enjoy a quality life.

The small-animal practitioner reveals that most canine breeds are subject to obesity, the exception being athletic sighthounds, such as Whippets, Borzois, Afghans and Greyhounds.

Sherman says that after the age of one, most cat and dog metabolic rates decrease, resulting in weight gain. The decreases continue as the animal gets older.

Since diet plays an important role in maintaining an animal's health, Sherman says that during a puppy or kitten's first visit to the veterinary hospital, staff members discuss balanced nutrition and acceptable treats with owners so the cat or dog can get a healthy start to what hopefully will be a long and healthy life.

"Owners should avoid feeding high-carb, high-fat foods to house pets with minimal physical activity," the veterinarian continues, adding that treats are a common contributor to obesity in companion animals.

"Most pets are food driven, and owners, in an attempt to please them, lavish them with treats," Sherman discloses. "It's hard to resist those big sad eyes and the begging behavior."

The veterinarian adds that treats are acceptable if the snacks are low in fat and carbohydrates and produced by a quality manufacturer. He adds that the focus on pet obesity has led some pet food companies to develop "lean" treats, which are a healthier alternative to richer foods.

Some dogs, Sherman says, enjoy an occasional fresh green bean or a piece of celery as a snack.

Just as humans shouldn't devour an entire bag of potato chips, pets should be offered treats only occasionally and in small amounts.

"Obesity in pets causes an increased load on joints and heart, advancing or causing progression of signs (symptoms) of heart disease or arthritic changes," Sherman discloses, adding that overweight pets with respiratory disease or other conditions with symptoms that include decreased oxygen delivery are also adversely affected by obesity.

According to Sherman, obesity can also be implicated in the development of diabetes, which requires a lot of effort to treat, and can be expensive as regular blood tests and medications are needed to control the disease.

Offering a glimmer of hope, Sherman emphasizes that although obesity is a serious health issue and owners must strive to keep their pets at a healthy weight, most diseases exacerbated by obesity can be improved by carefully controlled gradual weight loss.

"Lack of exercise and overfeeding is the cause of the obesity epidemic in pets," Sherman re-emphasizes, adding that dogs, if physically able with no underlying medical conditions, should be encouraged to run and walk regularly, except in extreme weather. Owners, in consultation with a veterinarian, need to create an exercise plan for brachiocephalic or short-nosed breeds, such as Pugs and French Bulldogs, as well as for elderly canines.

Felines should be offered safe cat toys and encouraged to play regularly with an adult or older child.

The veterinarian urges owners of obese pets to start exercise regimens slowly and, if the veterinarian approves, to gradually increase the amount of daily activity as the animal regains its vitality.

"The benefits of exercise are the same for people," Sherman concludes, listing calorie loss, strengthened muscles and improved mental health as just a few of the many advantages of keeping the family cat or dog in good physical condition.

BOYKIN SPANIEL A TRUE SOUTHERN TREASURE

If you are a true American patriot and like sporting dogs, the Boykin Spaniel might the perfect choice if you're searching for an ideal family canine companion.

These friendly, small hunters are just as comfortable stretched out on the living room rug as they are working in a swamp, and are valued for their keen intelligence, loyalty and friendly disposition.

The Boykin was developed at the beginning of the 20th Century by sportsmen to hunt wild turkeys in the Wateree River Swamp in South Carolina, where the breed was named the official state dog in 1985. The dogs also successfully adapt to dove fields and duck swamps, and today are prized by performance enthusiasts because they excel in agility, rally and other activities.

"They seem to be the breed of the hour," begins Paisley Stevens Knudsen, president of the Boykin Spaniel Club and Breeders Association of America, Inc. The Boykin Spaniel became eligible to be exhibited in the sporting group on January 1, 2008 and continues to attract a lot of media attention.

Knudsen estimates that although there are 10,000 Boykins scattered throughout the world, the heaviest concentration of the dogs remains in the Deep South.

According to Knudsen, the breed's origin can be traced to a small dog found wandering near a church in Spartanburg, South Carolina. It was adopted as a pet by Alexander White, who was attending services. White sent the canine to his hunting partner, L. Whittaker Boykin, a resident of a small rural agricultural community located on the outskirts of Camden, and the former stray developed into a superb turkey dog and waterfowl retriever.

154

Knudsen says although there are many opinions about some of the Boykin's other ancestors, most breed enthusiasts agree that the Field, Sussex, English Springer and field Cocker Spaniels, along with the Chesapeake Bay Retriever, all played a significant role in the new breed's development.

Since Boykins were smaller than a Labrador or Curly Coated Retriever, the animals could easily accompany sportsmen and became known as "the breed that wouldn't rock the boat."

Male specimens should measure between 15½ to 18 inches at the withers and never exceed 40 pounds, and females should stand between 14 and 16½ inches at the shoulder and weigh about 25 pounds.

"They are fabulous companions and family pets," Knudsen reveals, adding that Boykins "need some kind of job" and continue to earn rally and agility titles, as well as high scores in spaniel hunt tests.

"It's rare that we see a Boykin Spaniel that does just one thing," she continues, adding that since the breed became eligible for the show ring last month, two specimens have already earned an AKC championship title.

Knudsen, a school psychologist, also noted that because Boykins are friendly and can be easily trained, the animals are excellent therapy dogs and often work in hospitals and other medical settings.

According to the breed standard, the Boykin Spaniel has a dense undercoat and a solid colored outer coat that may be flat or slightly wavy, and rich liver, chocolate or brown.

"They are wash and wear dogs," Knudsen says. She adds that these loyal spaniels "just need a little scissoring" to clean footpads and private areas, and to trim the dog's face and docked tail. Unlike many breeds with long ears, Boykins aren't prone to infections, but ears should always be cleaned and nails trimmed to prevent infections.

"We don't face a lot of the obstacles that many of the flushing spaniels have," Knudsen notes, such as rage syndrome, a form of aggression sometimes found in certain bloodlines of English Springer Spaniels. The dog fancier adds that Boykins have even temperaments and are good with other dogs and children.

"They don't break," she quips. "They are like Tonka trucks."

She adds that these although these dogs thrive when they are engaged in any kind of activity and shouldn't be left to find their own amusement, Boykins are "adaptable" and can live harmoniously in the city as well as in the country.

Knudsen reports that although a well-bred specimen costs between $1,000 and $1,500, many healthy dogs with sound temperaments are available from Boykin Spaniel Rescue, Inc., a nonprofit organization whose members are committed to finding good homes for abandoned spaniels. For more information, visit www.boykinrescue.org.

"It's a 'Made in America' breed, " Knudsen concludes. "I think there's a Boykin for every household."

To learn more about the Boykin Spaniel, visit the American Kennel Club website at www.akc.org.

MEET THE GORDON SETTER—THE PRIDE OF SCOTLAND

If you want to put a smile on Susan Linhares' face, just start talking about dog shows, field trials and Gordon Setters.

The Mattapoisett, Massachusetts resident admits that although she's always loved sporting dogs, it's the handsome black and tan colored setter that stole her heart almost two decades ago.

"I just fell in love with the Gordon," Linhares begins, adding that as a child, her family owned English Setters. After she was married, she and her husband Frank, a truck driver who also loves dogs, bred English Springer Spaniels for field work, but eventually stopped breeding when they became concerned with the health and temperament issues that troubled the popular breed.

"I was looking for a versatile breed, a dog that could do it all," Linhares continues, describing herself as a "research junkie" and history buff who loves to read.

After devouring a wealth of material about sporting breeds, and armed with a vast knowledge of the other setter cousins — the popular Irish, equally handsome English, and the rugged Irish Red and White — Linhares decided to look for a Gordon Setter puppy.

"I went back to the breed that I'd always loved," she reveals. One day, the enthusiastic dog fancier discovered an issue of *Dog Fancy* magazine that was devoted to the Gordon and featured a centerfold photograph of one of these versatile setters that often stand out in the conformation ring and excel in performance events.

"The photograph was just stunning," Linhares recalls, adding that she had the image framed and proudly displayed it in her home.

Meanwhile, a friend who trained at the Plymouth County Canine Club, where Linhares was secretary for seven years, knew that the sporting dog fancier was searching for a Gordon Setter. One night, he showed her a classified newspaper advertisement offering a female Gordon puppy.

"I told him I didn't want that," Linhares admits, noting that she was searching for a puppy from a show kennel that produced healthy, versatile dogs, one "that could do it all."

Eventually curiosity got the best of the dog lover and she called the advertiser, who told her that the puppy was show quality and sired by the dog pictured in the magazine centerfold.

"I hounded the breeder until she sold the puppy to me," Linhares admits, laughing.

The rest is history.

That puppy became Ch. Pineridge Remember Rose, a beautiful Gordon that in addition to winning a conformation title, also earned a Companion Dog obedience degree and Canine Good Citizen title.

"Rosie" was honored by the Gordon Setter Club of America with the Beauty, Brains and Bird Sense Award for her many accomplishments. The versatile setter also produced 10 puppies that became AKC champions and was twice named "Brood Bitch of the Year" by the national club.

"She was everything I was looking for," Linhares recalls. "I will be forever grateful that I took a chance and called that telephone number."

Breed historians report that the Gordon Setter, a native of Scotland, was developed in the early 17th century by hunters, and gained prominence about 200 years later in the kennels owned by the fourth Duke of Gordon. Sportsmen prize the breed for its endurance, keen intelligence and retentive memory.

The Gordon is heavier than the other setters, and its luxurious black and tan colored coat can easily be seen by hunters in the field or when light snow covers the ground.

Linhares emphasizes that although she breeds to achieve sound temperaments and dogs that conform to the breed standard, it's also important that a Gordon Setter be able to hunt.

"I want to breed a dog that an owner can do anything with," she adds, noting that her Holly Hollow Kennels has produced more than 20 confirmation champions, and dogs that have earned 22 junior hunter, one senior and one master hunter titles.

"They bond very closely with their family," Linhares says of the loyal dogs, noting that the Gordon can play for hours with a toy and doesn't tend to run around the house like its red-colored Irish cousin.

Like most dogs, the Gordon Setter requires daily brushing and regular baths. Linhares, who currently keeps four dogs at the kennel, bathes dogs being exhibited every three days, trims footpads, and uses clippers to trim the top third of the dogs' ears and throat down to the chest bone to keep the animals in show condition.

Remarkably, Linhares underwent major neurological surgery five years ago and returned to the show ring late last year.

"I never thought I'd do it again," she said, adding that although she actively bred Gordons before her illness, she also worked as a professional handler and exhibited many other breeds.

Linhares said she became scared last November after entering her first dog show in many years, thinking that she'd drop the lead or fall, but her first venture back in the ring was a success.

"Everything just came back naturally," she concluded, adding that her friends' encouragement, husband's support and the unconditional love offered by her handsome Gordon Setters all helped her as she journeyed along the road to recovery.

COMBATING HEARTWORM DISEASE

Veterinarians are urging owners to have their cats and dogs checked for heartworm and to take precautions to prevent the disease from infecting the family pet.

Many different species of mosquitoes transmit heartworm, and over the years the disease has become a more prevalent problem in Northern latitudes. These pesky insects are starting to emerge as a result of the unusually warm spring and recent warm weather the region has experienced, so small-animal practitioners advise pet owners — even those who own indoor cats — to take the necessary steps to safeguard their four-footed companions against heartworm or to treat the disease in the aftermath of infection.

According to Dr. Nandini Jayaram, a veterinarian at Capeway Veterinary Hospital in Fairhaven, Massachusetts, the parasite or "worm" carried by the mosquito migrates through the tissues of the animal's body, and then settles in the blood vessels of the lungs and the right side of the heart.

"Heartworm is a very preventable disease," begins Dr. Thomas Burns of Veterinary Associates of Cape Cod in South Yarmouth, Massachusetts. "Obviously it is much better for a dog never to get heartworm; the damage to the heart, lungs, and other organs such as the liver can be permanent."

Burns says it's important that dogs and cats be placed on a regimen of preventative medication. Although dogs have been traditionally treated with a monthly pill, the respected veterinarian reveals that all too often the treatment plan becomes ineffective when owners forget to administer the medication.

An alternative is an injection that lasts six months and costs about the same as the monthly oral medication. Burns notes that there are also reminder e-mails sent by the veterinary clinic and "apps", software applications that send a message to a mobile device such as a cell phone or iPad, that helps owners remember to give preventative medications.

Jayaram adds that heartworm disease usually occurs when there has been a gap in prevention, such as when an owner skips treatment during the winter months because they think it's too cold for mosquitoes.

Burns said that although there is no heartworm treatment for cats, it's important that felines — especially those allowed outdoors — also receive preventative medication. Cats can be treated with a monthly topical application instead of a pill, something that most fussy felines and their owners appreciate.

The small-animal practitioner reports that many cases of heartworm are diagnosed during routine blood tests, which often also screens dogs for diseases transmitted by ticks, such as Lyme disease. Cats, he adds, are rarely screened for these illnesses.

"Testing is critical because it helps us find the heartworm before it becomes advanced, enabling us to treat the animal while it is still healthy, giving the patient a much better prognosis," Burns says, adding that it can take several years before heartworm is clinically noticeable.

Unfortunately, by the time an owner notices signs of the disease, it is often already in an advanced and critical stage and the canine is very sick. Dogs with advanced heartworm display symptoms such as coughing, shortness of breath and fatigue. If the disease is not promptly treated, it can cause organ failure and death.

"Severely infected dogs can die suddenly during exercise or exertion," Burns warns.

The popular veterinarian notes although heartworm disease is much more common in dogs than cats, the disease rate in felines is much higher than most experts recognize.

"Clinical signs of heartworm in cats are often much more subtle, or misinterpreted as other conditions such as asthma or heart failure," Burns notes, adding that the disease is much more difficult to diagnose in felines, partly because the testing is more extensive and less reliable. One study, he reports, found that upwards of 15 percent of indoor cats have been exposed to heartworm disease in certain regions.

According to Jayaram, signs of advanced heartworm disease include coughing, vomiting and weight loss.

"Unfortunately, sudden death does occur in a fair number of cats, thought to be due to blood clots caused by the disease," she discloses. "Owners of both dogs and cats should be vigilant for any signs of respiratory disease."

Jayaram thinks that recent climatic trends toward warmer, wetter, "mosquito friendly" weather and milder winters will lead to an increase in heartworm disease in Southern New England if owners fail to take preventable measures.

The small-animal practitioner adds that compounding the problem is the fact that the availability of the most effective drug used to treat the disease is currently limited because of a scarcity of the raw materials required to manufacture the pharmaceutical.

"There has also been data showing that cross-state movement of dogs for adoption purposes has led to the spread of disease in areas where heartworm was previously very low," Jayaram reveals. "This was found to be true especially after Hurricane Katrina, when many dogs from the Gulf area, where heartworm is endemic due to the weather conditions, were sent to shelters up north."

Michael Patnaude, a senior research biologist at Smithers Viscient Laboratories in Wareham, urges pet owners to remove standing water from birdbaths and containers where rainwater can collect. These areas become prime breeding grounds for mosquitoes.

Noting that there are 26 species of the pesky insects that carry heartworm, Patnaude, like both veterinarians, urges pet owners to remain vigilant throughout the year.

"They are all out at different times," he concludes.

AUSTRALIAN CATTLE DOG EXCELS AT AGILITY

The Australian Cattle Dog has been prized by farmers and owners across the globe for more than two centuries for its loyalty and diligence, and continues to attract fans in the United States because of the breed's intelligence and ability to excel at performance events.

Last year, this hardworking herding breed, which was developed in its native land in the early 1800s to assist cattle farmers on large tracts of land, ranked 59th in popularity according to American Kennel Club statistics, and is slowly being discovered by people who seek a versatile working dog and devoted family companion.

Bourne, Massachusetts resident Kelly McNiff became interested in the breed in 2001 when she acquired an ACD-mix as a pet. She later adopted a purebred male, and now owns Bella, an eight-year-old female who has achieved success in obedience, and Twister, a handsome five-year-old male who has won accolades in the conformation ring and is working on earning rally, agility and obedience titles.

McNiff recalls that once she became hooked on the breed, she contacted some of the leading kennels in Australia, but discovered that the cost of purchasing a puppy plus shipping would be prohibitive. Breeders there suggested that she contact an American kennel with Australian bloodlines.

"I didn't expect to buy a puppy right away," McNiff begins. "When Twister came up, I just couldn't walk away from him."

The cattle dog fan recalls viewing pictures of Twister's litter on the Internet, and says that she couldn't take her eyes off of the handsome blue-speckled dog.

"I just keep getting drawn back to him," she continues, adding that Twister, officially known as Austlyn's Heading for the Cape, quickly won her heart.

According to breed historians, the Australian Cattle Dog was developed in the early 19th century by cattle ranchers by crossing imported collie-like stock with indigenous dogs, including the Dingo. It's also believed that Dalmatians were later used to develop a breed that would be equally as comfortable around horses as it was nipping heels and keeping large herds of cattle together on the grassy plains.

"They have a serious temperament," McNiff explains, describing the canines as "self-thinkers.

"You can see them work things out in their heads," she says. "They are high energy and active."

Although describing Twister as a "lovebug," McNiff adds that these dogs can be very reserved when approached by strangers. Breed fanciers often refer to the ACD as "the Velcro dog" because the loyal animals often tend to select one family member and seldom leave that person's side.

McNiff adds that like any breed, cattle dogs need training and a job or they'll become destructive and the living room sofa will be soon torn to shreds.

"They have to go out and do things," she continues, noting that Twister loves agility, and will have an opportunity to run through the challenging obstacle course and accomplish other feats next week at the Cape Cod Kennel Club's Spring Agility Trials, to be held June 14, 15 and 16, 8 a.m. to 4 p.m., outdoors on the grass, at the Barnstable County Fairgrounds in Falmouth. Admission is free.

According to the AKC, agility is a performance event in which a handler directs a dog through an obstacle course in a race for both time and accuracy. The canine runs off-leash with no food or toys offered as incentives, and the handler can touch neither the dog nor the obstacles, which are laid out on a course designed by the officiating judge.

Consequently the handler's controls are limited to voice, movement, and various body signals, requiring exceptional training of the animal and coordination of the handler.

The obstacles include an A-frame, a dog walk, a teeter-totter, tunnels, jumps and weave poles.

According to David Wyndham, the club's agility chairman, the athletic activity forges an unbreakable bond between a dog and its handler.

Wyndham, who owns two Briards — a breed developed in France to herd flocks of sheep and guard its master's property — adds that although sporting and herding breeds naturally excel in agility, any dog that is properly trained by a patient owner can succeed.

"I've seen Chihuahuas and Great Danes and everything in between," he says, adding that some breeds, such as Border Collies and Golden Retrievers are naturally athletic, but terriers, which were developed to work independently, can be more difficult to train.

Wyndham says that when he finishes a course and his dog is eager to start all over again, it makes the hard work and extensive training all worthwhile. He encourages spectators interested in performance activities to attend the trials to discover the fun-filled sport. Experts and owners will be on hand to answer questions about getting started in the sport.

"It's a good opportunity to see owners working with their dogs," Wyndham emphasizes. "You can see that the dogs are having fun."

According to AKC rules, only dogs entered in the competition are allowed on the event grounds.

For more information about the trials or agility classes sponsored by the Cape Cod Kennel Club, call **(774)** 327-0539.

ABOUT THE AUTHOR

Brian J. Lowney is a past president of the Wampanoag Kennel Club in Massachusetts, and an AKC licensed judge of Junior Showmanship classes. He is a weekly newspaper pet columnist and has covered many different beats during his long career as a journalist.

CPSIA information can be obtained at www.ICGtesting.com
Printed in the USA
BVOW07s1206250913

332084BV00009B/438/P